EXPLORing AUSTIN with Kids

ANNETTE LUCKSINGER

Over **100** Fun Things to Do with the Family

Stomping Grounds
PRESS

Copyright © 2014 by Annette Lucksinger
Published by Stomping Grounds Press
Austin, Texas

ISBN 978-0-9912270-0-6

Find us on the Internet at: www.ExploringAustinwithKids.com
For general inquiries: info@ExploringAustinwithKids.com

Edited by Annette Lucksinger with Jodi Egerton of Write Good Consulting
Cover and interior design by Monica Thomas for TLC Graphics, www.TLCGraphics.com

Royalty-free illustrations are from various contributors for Dreamstime.com.

COVER: City © Tasia12; Hand © Viola Di Pietro; Magnifying glass © Digiselector; Dinosaur © Petr Novotny; Food truck © Rceeh; Picture frame © Nataliashein **ICONS:** Bulb © Igor Dudáš; Slide © Andre Adams; Shoe © Ofchina; Purse © Anatolii Cojuhari; Food © Alevtina Karro; Globe © Dedmazay; Tree and bike © Notkoo2008; Flip flops © Elfivetrov; Van © Roberto Giovannini **INDEXES:** Kites © Oleksandr Melnyk; Map © Iryna Dobrovyns'ka; Airplane © Torky; Compass © Kytalpa; Tracks © Ievgen Soloviov; Piggy bank © Vladimir Yudin; Calendar © Natashasha **MAP:** Trees © Yuliia Brykova; Binoculars © Popcic; Restroom & picnic table © Candi4636; Hiking boot © Michael Mcdonald; Swimming mask © Rainledy. Many illustrations were modified by Monica Thomas.

First Edition

Printed in the United States of America

~To my fellow explorers~
Daniel, Emmi, and Stone

Table of Contents

Introduction

This guidebook highlights activities and events that appeal not only to kids of all ages but also to the fun-loving grown-ups that accompany them. Those new to parenting will find it a guide into the entirely new city that appears with the birth of a first child. Experienced Austin parents will discover fresh, new places yet to be explored. Visitors will find it invaluable in leading to the must-see tourist destinations and the popular local haunts that make Austin such a vibrant city.

Austin has no shortage of family-friendly activities and events. Included are those that best exemplify the spirit of the city to:

> ➤ Get outdoors

> ➤ Support local enterprise

> ➤ Celebrate the arts and culture

> ➤ Enjoy the unique, fun places that "Keep Austin Weird."

To help identify outings best suited to your family, the Table of Contents arranges entries categorically by age, location, and activity type.

How to use this book

New Parents

On the day your first child is born, the city magically changes. Doors open to places you never considered visiting as you come to look forward to trips to the zoo, movies surrounded by babies, and outdoor performances by children's musicians. The city becomes fun all over again.

To help ease your way into this child culture:

➤ See the "Baby" entries listed in the Table of Contents for some good spots for getting out.

➤ The "Places to Wander" section also offers suggestions for low stress outings for parents and little ones to explore the world together.

➤ Later you can graduate to the "Toddler/Preschool" favorites. From there, your child's interests will likely influence the activities you choose and the places you go.

Experienced Austin Parents

If you are a parent with plenty of Austin experience under your belt, this book can lead you to yet unexplored places and make it simpler to visit those you have been wanting to see. Here are some tips for how to best use this guide:

➤ Toss it in the car or stroller and keep it there for easy reference as you head out to explore. The Table of Contents can help pinpoint activities by age, interest, and location. A monthly Events Calendar will also keep you up to date on festivals and annual events.

➤ Download the mobile app *(see the Additional Resources section)* to make it easy to find the nearest fun. You might be surprised by the number of unexpected treasures just streets over from your typical routes through the city.

➤ Explore someone else's backyard. Likely, you have a number of favorite haunts in a particular swath of the city, but try a new park, library, swimming hole, restaurant, or trail in a different part of town. Branching out a bit can be exciting as you discover the diversity of experience the city has to offer.

Visitors

In planning your trip to the capital city, be sure to check the list of "Top Tourist Destinations" that will direct your family to those uniquely

Austin experiences. If you have the time and inclination, there are also plenty of quirky places off the beaten path. In a fun-loving city that embraces the outdoors, live music, and local culture as Austin does, there is always much to see and do. To help you narrow things down:

➤ The Table of Contents can help plan fitting activities by area or by your children's ages and interests.

➤ Download the mobile app *(see the Additional Resources section)* to make it easy to pinpoint restaurants, parks, and events close to your destinations.

➤ Each year Austin hosts numerous festivals that are fun for families, often several on any given weekend. Check the Events Calendar for the dates that coincide with your visit.

Icons

Look for these icons alongside each entry. They will give you a quick sense of the activities you can expect to find at each place. Cross-references are noted in bold, italicized font within the entries.

Activity Icon Key

Educational	Shopping
Active	Food/Treats
Cultural	Museum
Entertainment	Outdoors
Playground	

Additional Resources

The resources section of this guide offers a select list of free local publications that contain weekly and monthly calendars to keep you informed of ongoing activities, camps, and classes. Kid-savvy blogs with daily deals and local events are also noted.

The mobile app *Exploring Austin with Kids* grants users full access to the guidebook's contents and allows searches by destination, activity type, age level, or nearby places.

The website *ExploringAustinwithKids.com* will provide you with:

➤ Updates to guidebook entries

➤ New places to explore

➤ Upcoming family fun events

➤ Austin trivia and interviews with local characters

➤ Photographs and insider tips

Safety

Texas can get downright hot in the spring and summer months. So set out in the morning before things warm up and take care to guard young ones from the heat. It's always good to be prepared and keep an "emergency bag" stashed in the car for potential mishaps too, from bee stings or poison ivy to downpours and unplanned dips in the creek. Here are some ideas for filling it:

Hats/baseball caps	Picnic blanket
Water bottles	Towel
Sunscreen	Spare clothes
Insect repellent	Rain gear/umbrellas
Antibacterial hand sanitizer	Flashlight
Emergency snacks	Lighter
Whistle	Pen and paper

Pocketknife (or scissors/bottle opener)

$5-10 bill and quarters (for unexpected parking, snacks, entrance fees)

First aid kit *(pre-packaged kits are available or put together your own)*:

Band-Aids	Tweezers
Gauze	Pain reliever
Disinfectant, hydrogen peroxide	Benadryl for allergic reactions
Triple antibiotic ointment	Hand cleansing wipes
Moleskin or "Second Skin" for blisters	

General Advice

Call ahead

Each entry lists the most up-to-date information available at the time of publication. However, Austin is a dynamic city and things are constantly changing. So call ahead or refer to your destination's website to verify hours and admission fees before you go.

Stay on the trail

Poison ivy is prevalent in these parts. Stick to the trails when hiking to avoid wandering off into a patch of it. If exposed, wash the area with soap and water as soon as possible.

Check the weather report

Be sure to check the forecast since Texas weather can change rather abruptly.

Get buy-in

Kids will enjoy the experience even more when they are involved in the planning. Let them help decide on outings, map the route, pack snacks, give directions, and take pictures once you get to your destination.

Have fun
Get out and enjoy!

Categorical List of Entries

Alphabetical List of Places

Alamo Drafthouse

Amy's Ice Creams

Ann and Roy Butler Hike and Bike Trail at Lady Bird Lake

Anna's Toy Depot

Austin Books and Comics

Austin Duck Adventures

Austin Independent School District Playgrounds

Austin Nature and Science Center in Zilker Park

Austin Public Libraries

Austin Steam Train

Austin Zoo

Barton Creek Farmers Market

Barton Creek Greenbelt

Barton Springs Pool in Zilker Park

Bat Watching

Big Top Candy Shop

Blanton Museum of Art

The Bob Bullock Texas State History Museum

Boggy Creek Farm

BookPeople

Bright Leaf Preserve

Butler Park

Camp Mabry

Capital MetroRail

Capital of Texas Zoo

Capitol Visitors Center

Casey's New Orleans Snowballs

Central Market

Chaparral Ice Skating

City of Austin Parks

City of Austin Pools and Splash Pads

The Contemporary Austin at Laguna Gloria

Crowe's Nest Farm

Dart Bowl

Deep Eddy Pool

Dinosaur Park

Doc's Backyard

Dougherty Arts Theater

Downtown Farmers' Market

Eco-Wise

Ella Wooten Pool at Mueller

Emma Long Metropolitan Park

Frank and Angie's Pizzeria

Freddie's Place

George Washington Carver Museum and Cultural Center

Green Mesquite BBQ

Hamilton Pool Preserve

Hideout Theatre—Flying Theater Machine Group

Hill Country Galleria Splash Pad

Hill's Café

Home Slice Pizza

Irving and Hazeline Smith Trail

Kiddie Acres

Krause Springs

Lady Bird Johnson Wildflower Center

Long Center

Lou Neff Point in Zilker Park

Matt's El Rancho

Mayfield Park and Preserve

McKinney Falls State Park

McKinney Roughs Nature Park

Mexic-Arte Museum

Millennium Youth Entertainment Complex

Mount Bonnell

Mueller Farmers' Market

Mueller Parks and Trails

Over the Rainbow

P. Terry's Burger Stand

Pedernales Falls State Park

Peter Pan Mini-Golf

Phil's Ice House

Pioneer Farms

Playland Skate Center

River Place Nature Trail

Rootin' Ridge

Round Rock Express Baseball

Rowing Dock in Zilker Park

St. Edward's Trail

Scottish Rite Children's Theater

Sno-Beach

Splash! Exhibit in Zilker Park

Stargazing at the Roughs

Sugar Mama's Bakeshop

Sunset Valley Farmers' and Artisans' Markets

Terra Toys

Texas Memorial Museum

Texas Rowing Center in Zilker Park

Texas State Capitol

Thinkery: The New Austin Children's Museum

Torchy's Tacos

Tower Garden

Toy Joy

Triangle Farmers' Market

Turkey Creek Trail

Umlauf Sculpture Garden in
Zilker Park

The Union Underground

University of Texas Tower Tour

Veloway

Walter E. Long Metropolitan
Park at Decker Lake

Westcave Outdoor Discovery
Center

Westcave Outdoor Discovery
Center Star Party

Whole Earth Provisions

Whole Foods Rooftop

Wild Basin Stargazing and
Moonlighting Tours

ZACH Theatre

Zilker Park

 Austin Nature and Science
 Center

 Barton Springs Pool

 Lou Neff Point

 Rowing Dock

 Splash! Exhibit

 Texas Rowing Center

 Umlauf Sculpture Garden

 Zilker Botanical Gardens

 Zilker Nature Preserve and
 Hiking Trails

 Zilker Park Boat Rentals

 Zilker Park Playscape

 Zilker Zephyr

Alphabetical List of Annual Events

Austin Dragon Boat Festival and Race

Austin Family Music Festival

Austin Museum Day

Austin Trail of Lights

Beverly S. Sheffield Zilker Hillside Theatre

Children's Day Art Park

Christmas Lights on 37th Street

Chuy's Children Giving to Children Parade

Crowe's Nest Farm Fall Family Fun Fest

Día de Los Muertos Viva La Vida Fest

Eeyore's Birthday Party

Explore UT

Holiday Sing-Along and Downtown Stroll

Ice Skating at Whole Foods

Juggle Fest

Lake Travis Hot Air Balloon Flyover

Luminations at Lady Bird Johnson Wildflower Center

Music Under the Star Concert Series

Muster Days at Camp Mabry

Nature Nights at Lady Bird Johnson Wildflower Center

Rodeo Austin

Shakespeare in the Park

Texas Book Festival

Zilker Holiday Tree

Zilker Kite Festival

Listings by Interest

The symbol **E** specifies that a listing is an annual event.

Airplanes
Camp Mabry
Kiddie Acres
Muster Days at Camp Mabry **E**

Animals
Austin Nature and Science Center in Zilker Park
Austin Zoo
Bat Watching
Boggy Creek Farm
Capital of Texas Zoo
Crowe's Nest Farm
Kiddie Acres
Lou Neff Point in Zilker Park
Mayfield Park and Preserve
Nature Nights at Lady Bird Johnson Wildflower Center **E**
Pioneer Farms

Rodeo Austin **E**
Tower Garden

Arts
Beverly S. Sheffield Zilker Hillside Theatre in Zilker Park **E**
Blanton Museum of Art
Children's Day Art Park **E**
The Contemporary Austin at Laguna Gloria
Día de Los Muertos Viva La Vida Fest **E**
Dougherty Arts Theater
Explore UT **E**
Hideout Theatre—Flying Theater Machine Group
Long Center
Mexic-Arte Museum
Scottish Rite Children's Theater
Shakespeare in the Park **E**
Umlauf Sculpture Garden in Zilker Park
ZACH Theatre

Biking
McKinney Falls State Park
Mueller Parks and Trails
Pedernales Falls State Park
Veloway

Birds
Amy's Ice Creams Arboretum

Austin Nature and Science Center in Zilker Park

Austin Zoo

Boggy Creek Farm

Capital of Texas Zoo

Central Market

Crowe's Nest Farm

Lou Neff Point

Mayfield Park and Preserve

Pedernales Falls State Park

Boats

Austin Dragon Boat Festival **E**

Austin Duck Adventures

Bat Watching

Kiddie Acres

Rowing Dock in Zilker Park

Texas Rowing Center in Zilker Park

Zilker Park Boat Rentals in Zilker Park

Books

Austin Books and Comics

Austin Public Libraries

BookPeople

Over the Rainbow

Terra Toys

Texas Book Festival **E**

Whole Earth Provisions

Bowling

Dart Bowl

Millennium Youth Entertainment Complex

The Union Underground

Camping

Emma Long Metropolitan Park

Krause Springs

McKinney Falls State Park

Pedernales Falls State Park

Creek Play

Barton Creek Greenbelt

City of Austin Parks

Irving and Hazeline Smith Trail

Lou Neff Point in Zilker Park

McKinney Falls State Park

Pedernales Falls State Park

River Place Nature Trail

St. Edward's Trail

Turkey Creek Trail

Zilker Nature Preserve and Hiking Trails

Cultural Centers and Events

Austin Dragon Boat Festival **E**

Día de Los Muertos Viva La Vida Fest **E**

George Washington Carver Museum and Cultural Center

Mexic-Arte Museum

Dinosaurs

Austin Nature and Science Center Dino Pit

Dinosaur Park

Texas Memorial Museum

Zilker Botanical Gardens Hartman Prehistoric Garden

Educational Centers and Events

Austin Nature and Science Center in Zilker Park

The Bob Bullock Texas State History Museum

Camp Mabry

Capitol Visitors Center

Crowe's Nest Farm

Dinosaur Park

Explore UT **E**

George Washington Carver Museum and Cultural Center

Lady Bird Johnson Wildflower Center

Nature Nights at Lady Bird Johnson Wildflower Center **E**

Splash! Exhibit in Zilker Park

Texas Memorial Museum

Thinkery: The New Austin Children's Museum

Farms

Boggy Creek Farm

Crowe's Nest Farm

Pioneer Farms

Farmers' Markets

Barton Creek Farmers Market

Boggy Creek Farm

Downtown Farmers' Market

Mueller Farmers' Market

Sunset Valley Farmers' and Artisans' Markets

Triangle Farmers' Market

Field Trips

Austin Duck Adventures

Austin Nature and Science Center in Zilker Park

Austin Zoo

Blanton Museum of Art

The Bob Bullock Texas State History Museum

Bright Leaf Preserve

Capital of Texas Zoo

Capitol Visitors Center

The Contemporary Austin at Laguna Gloria

Crowe's Nest Farm

Dinosaur Park

Explore UT **E**

Long Center

Pioneer Farms

Texas Memorial Museum

Texas State Capitol

Thinkery: The New Austin Children's Museum

ZACH Theatre

Zilker Park

Fishing

Camp Mabry

Emma Long Metropolitan Park

McKinney Falls State Park

Mueller Parks and Trails

Walter E. Long Metropolitan Park at Decker Lake

Hiking Trails

Austin Nature and Science Center in Zilker Park

Barton Creek Greenbelt

Bright Leaf Preserve

Hamilton Pool Preserve

Irving and Hazeline Smith Trail

Lady Bird Johnson Wildflower Center

Mayfield Park and Preserve

McKinney Falls State Park

McKinney Roughs Nature Park

Mount Bonnell

Pedernales Falls State Park

River Place Nature Trail

St. Edward's Trail

Turkey Creek Trail

Westcave Outdoor Discovery Center

Wild Basin

Zilker Nature Preserve and Hiking Trails

History

Austin Duck Adventures

Austin Steam Train

The Bob Bullock Texas State History Museum

Camp Mabry

Capitol Visitors Center

George Washington Carver Museum and Cultural Center

Muster Days at Camp Mabry **E**

Pioneer Farms

Texas Memorial Museum

Texas State Capitol

Zilker Botanical Gardens Pioneer Settlement

Ice Skating

Chaparral Ice Skating

Whole Foods Ice Skating (seasonal) **E**

Live Children's Entertainment

Austin Family Music Festival **E**

Austin Public Libraries

Beverly S. Sheffield Zilker Hillside Theatre in Zilker Park **E**

Children's Day Art Park **E**

Dougherty Arts Theater

Hideout Theatre—Flying Theater Machine Group

Juggle Fest **E**

Long Center

Rodeo Austin **E**

Scottish Rite Children's Theater

Texas Book Festival **E**

ZACH Theatre

Live Music

Austin Family Music Festival **E**

Barton Creek Farmers Market

Central Market

Children's Day Art Park **E**

Día de Los Muertos Viva La Vida Fest **E**

Doc's Backyard

Downtown Farmers' Market

Freddie's Place

Green Mesquite BBQ

Long Center

Mueller Farmers' Market

Music Under the Star Concert Series **E**

Sunset Valley Farmers' and Artisans' Markets

Triangle Farmers' Market

Movies

Alamo Drafthouse

Austin Public Libraries

Bob Bullock Texas State History Museum IMAX and Texas Spirit Theaters

Deep Eddy Splash Party Movie Nights **E**

Long Center Movies on the Lawn **E**

Millennium Youth Entertainment Complex

Museums

Blanton Museum of Art

Bob Bullock Texas State History Museum

Camp Mabry Texas Military Forces Museum

Capitol Visitors Center

The Contemporary Austin at Laguna Gloria

George Washington Carver Museum and Cultural Center

Mexic-Arte Museum

Pioneer Farms

Texas Memorial Museum

Thinkery: The New Austin Children's Museum

Umlauf Sculpture Garden in Zilker Park

Parks

Butler Park

City of Austin Parks

Emma Long Metropolitan Park

Mayfield Park and Preserve

McKinney Falls State Park

McKinney Roughs Nature Park

Mueller Parks and Trails

Pedernales Falls State Park

Walter E. Long Metropolitan Park at Decker Lake

Zilker Park

Places to Wander

Austin Nature and Science Center in Zilker Park

Butler Park

The Contemporary Austin at Laguna Gloria

Lady Bird Johnson Wildflower Center

Mayfield Park and Preserve

Texas State Capitol

Umlauf Sculpture Garden in Zilker Park

Zilker Botanical Gardens

Zilker Park

Playgrounds

Austin Independent School District Playgrounds

Central Market Playscape

City of Austin Parks

Doc's Backyard

Freddie's Place

Mueller Parks and Trails

Phil's Ice House/Amy's Ice Creams

Whole Foods Rooftop

Zilker Park Playscape

Restaurants

Central Market

Doc's Backyard

Frank and Angie's Pizzeria

Freddie's Place

Green Mesquite BBQ

Hill's Café

Home Slice Pizza

Matt's El Rancho

P. Terry's Burger Stand

Phil's Ice House

Torchy's Tacos

Whole Foods Rooftop

Roller Skating

Millennium Youth Entertainment Complex

Playland Skate Center

Sand Play

Austin Nature and Science Center Dino Pit

Dinosaur Park

Emma Long Metropolitan Park

Mueller Parks and Trails

P. Terry's Burger Stand

Zilker Park Playscape

Science

Austin Nature and Science Center in Zilker Park

Explore UT **E**

McKinney Roughs Nature Park

Nature Nights at Lady Bird Johnson Wildflower Center **E**

Splash! Exhibit in Zilker Park

Stargazing at the Roughs

Texas Memorial Museum

Thinkery: The New Austin Children's Museum

Westcave Outdoor Discovery Center Star Party

Whole Earth Provisions

Wild Basin Stargazing and Moonlighting Tours

Splash Pads

Butler Park

City of Austin Pools and Splash Pads

Hill Country Galleria Splash Pad

Triangle Farmers' Market

Sports

Chaparral Ice Skating

Dart Bowl

Kiddie Acres Miniature Golf

Millennium Youth Entertainment Complex

Peter Pan Mini-Golf

Playland Skate Center

Round Rock Express

Rowing Dock

Texas Rowing Center

The Union Underground

Whole Foods Ice Skating (seasonal) **E**

Zilker Park Boat Rentals

Stargazing

Stargazing at the Roughs

Westcave Outdoor Discovery Center Star Party

Wild Basin Stargazing and Moonlighting Tours

Storytimes

Austin Public Libraries

The Bob Bullock Texas State History Museum

BookPeople

Thinkery: The New Austin Children's Museum

Swimming

Barton Creek Greenbelt

Barton Springs Pool in Zilker Park

City of Austin Pools and Splash Pads

Deep Eddy Pool

Ella Wooten Pool at Mueller

Emma Long Metropolitan Park

Hamilton Pool Preserve

Krause Springs

McKinney Falls State Park

Pedernales Falls State Park

Walter E. Long Metropolitan Park at Decker Lake

Theatre

Beverly S. Sheffield Zilker Hillside Theatre in Zilker Park **E**

Dougherty Arts Theater

Hideout Theatre—Flying Theater Machine Group

Long Center

Scottish Rite Children's Theater

Shakespeare in the Park in Zilker Park **E**

ZACH Theatre

Top Tourist Destinations

Austin Duck Adventures

Austin Nature and Science Center in Zilker Park

Bat Watching

Big Top Candy Shop

The Bob Bullock Texas State History Museum

Texas State Capitol

Thinkery: The New Austin Children's Museum

Zilker Park

Zilker Zephyr

Tours

Austin Duck Adventures

Bat Watching

Bright Leaf Preserve
Capitol Visitors Center
McKinney Falls State Park
McKinney Roughs Nature Park
Texas State Capitol
University of Texas Tower Tour
Westcave Outdoor Discovery
  Center
Wild Basin Stargazing and
  Moonlighting Tours

Toys

Anna's Toy Depot
Eco-Wise
Over the Rainbow
Rootin' Ridge
Terra Toys
Toy Joy
Whole Earth Provisions

Trains

Austin Steam Train
Austin Zoo
Capital MetroRail
Kiddie Acres
Zilker Zephyr

Treats

Amy's Ice Creams
Big Top Candy Shop

Casey's New Orleans Snowballs
Sno-Beach
Sugar Mama's Bakeshop

Zilker Park

Ann and Roy Butler Hike and
  Bike Trail at Lady Bird Lake
Austin Nature and Science
  Center
Austin Trail of Lights **E**
Barton Springs Pool
Beverly S. Sheffield Zilker
  Hillside Theatre **E**
Lou Neff Point
Rowing Dock
Splash! Exhibit
Texas Rowing Center
Umlauf Sculpture Garden
Zilker Botanical Gardens
Zilker Holiday Tree **E**
Zilker Kite Festival **E**
Zilker Nature Preserve and
  Hiking Trails
Zilker Park Boat Rentals
Zilker Park Playscape
Zilker Zephyr

Zoos

Austin Zoo
Capital of Texas Zoo

Listings by Age

Baby

Annual Events
Austin Dragon Boat Festival

Austin Trail of Lights

Christmas Lights on 37th Street

Texas Book Festival

Zilker Holiday Tree

Zilker Kite Festival

Food & Drink
Amy's Ice Creams

Central Market—north location

Doc's Backyard

Frank and Angie's Pizzeria

Freddie's Place

Green Mesquite BBQ

Hill's Café

Matt's El Rancho

Phil's Ice House

Sugar Mama's Bakeshop

Torchy's Tacos

Whole Foods Rooftop

Outings
Alamo Drafthouse Tuesday Baby Days

Ann and Roy Butler Hike and Bike Trail at Lady Bird Lake

Austin Public Libraries and Baby Storytimes

Austin Zoo

Barton Creek Farmers Market

Boggy Creek Farm

Capital of Texas Zoo

Central Market

City of Austin Parks

City of Austin Pools and Splash Pads

The Contemporary Austin at Laguna Gloria

Deep Eddy Pool

Downtown Farmers' Market

Ella Wooten Pool at Mueller

Mayfield Park and Preserve

Mueller Farmers' Market

Mueller Parks and Trails

Sunset Valley Farmers' and Artisans' Markets

Texas State Capitol Lawn

Thinkery: The New Austin Children's Museum

Triangle Farmers' Market

Umlauf Sculpture Garden in Zilker Park

Zilker Botanical Gardens

Zilker Nature Preserve and Hiking Trails

Zilker Park

Zilker Park Playscape

Zilker Zephyr

Products

Anna's Toy Depot

BookPeople

Eco-Wise

Over the Rainbow

Rootin' Ridge

Terra Toys

Whole Earth Provisions

Toddler/Preschooler

Annual Events

Austin Dragon Boat Festival

Austin Family Music Festival

Austin Museum Day

Austin Trail of Lights

Children's Day Art Park

Christmas Lights on 37th Street

Chuy's Children Giving to Children Parade

Crowe's Nest Farm Fall Family Fun Fest

Día de Los Muertos Viva La Vida Fest

Eeyore's Birthday Party

Explore UT

Holiday Sing-Along and Downtown Stroll

Juggle Fest

Lake Travis Hot Air Balloon Flyover

Luminations at Lady Bird Johnson Wildflower Center

Music Under the Star Concert Series

Muster Days at Camp Mabry

Nature Nights at Lady Bird Johnson Wildflower Center

Rodeo Austin

Texas Book Festival

Zilker Holiday Tree

Zilker Kite Festival

Food & Drink

Amy's Ice Creams

Big Top Candy Shop

Casey's New Orleans Snowballs

Central Market

Doc's Backyard

Frank and Angie's Pizzeria

Freddie's Place

Home Slice Pizza

Matt's El Rancho

P. Terry's Burger Stand

Phil's Ice House

Sno-Beach

Sugar Mama's Bakeshop

Torchy's Tacos

Whole Foods Rooftop

Fun Places to Shop

Anna's Toy Depot

BookPeople

Over the Rainbow

Rootin' Ridge

Terra Toys

Whole Earth Provisions

Outings

Austin Independent School District Playgrounds

Austin Nature and Science Center in Zilker Park

Austin Public Libraries

Austin Steam Train: Day Out with Thomas & Polar Express

Austin Zoo

Barton Creek Greenbelt

The Bob Bullock Texas State History Museum: TEXploration Family Story Times

Boggy Creek Farm

Butler Park

Capital MetroRail

Capital of Texas Zoo

City of Austin Parks

City of Austin Pools and Splash Pads

The Contemporary Austin at Laguna Gloria

Crowe's Nest Farm

Deep Eddy Pool

Dinosaur Park

Dougherty Arts Theater

Downtown Farmers' Market

Ella Wooten Pool at Mueller

Emma Long Metropolitan Park

Hideout Theatre—Flying Theater Machine Group

Hill Country Galleria Splash Pad

Irving and Hazeline Smith Trail

Kiddie Acres

Lady Bird Johnson Wildflower Center

Long Center

Lou Neff Point in Zilker Park

Mueller Farmers' Market

Mayfield Park and Preserve

Mueller Parks and Trails

River Place Nature Trail

Scottish Rite Children's Theater

Splash! Exhibit in Zilker Park

Sunset Valley Farmers' and Artisans' Markets

Texas Memorial Museum

Thinkery: The New Austin Children's Museum

Tower Garden

Triangle Farmers' Market

Umlauf Sculpture Garden in Zilker Park

ZACH Theatre

Zilker Botanical Gardens

Zilker Nature Preserve and Hiking Trails

Zilker Park

Zilker Park Playscape

Zilker Zephyr

Grade School (ages 5-9)

Annual Events

Austin Dragon Boat Festival

Austin Family Music Festival

Austin Museum Day

Austin Trail of Lights

Beverly S. Sheffield Zilker Hillside Theatre

Children's Day Art Park

Christmas Lights on 37th Street

Chuy's Children Giving to Children Parade

Crowe's Nest Farm Fall Family Fun Fest

Día de Los Muertos Viva La Vida Fest

Eeyore's Birthday Party

Explore UT

Holiday Sing-Along and Downtown Stroll

Ice Skating at Whole Foods

Juggle Fest

Lake Travis Hot Air Balloon Flyover

Luminations at Lady Bird Johnson Wildflower Center

Music Under the Star Concert Series

Muster Days at Camp Mabry

Nature Nights at Lady Bird Johnson Wildflower Center

Rodeo Austin

Texas Book Festival

Zilker Holiday Tree

Zilker Kite Festival

Food & Drink

Amy's Ice Creams

Big Top Candy Shop

Casey's New Orleans Snowballs

Central Market

Doc's Backyard

Frank and Angie's Pizzeria

Freddie's Place

Green Mesquite BBQ

Hill's Café

Home Slice Pizza

Matt's El Rancho

P. Terry's Burger Stand

Phil's Ice House

Sno-Beach

Sugar Mama's Bakeshop

Torchy's Tacos

Whole Foods Rooftop

Fun Places to Shop

Anna's Toy Depot

Austin Books and Comics

BookPeople

Eco-Wise

Hill Country Galleria

Over the Rainbow

Rootin' Ridge

Terra Toys

Toy Joy

Whole Earth Provisions

Outings

Alamo Drafthouse

Austin Duck Adventures

Austin Independent School District Playgrounds

Austin Nature and Science Center in Zilker Park

Austin Public Libraries

Austin Steam Train

Austin Zoo

Barton Creek Farmers Market

Barton Creek Greenbelt

Barton Springs Pool in Zilker Park

Bat Watching

The Bob Bullock Texas State History Museum

Boggy Creek Farm

Butler Park

Camp Mabry

Capital MetroRail

Capital of Texas Zoo

Capitol Visitors Center

Chaparral Ice Skating

City of Austin Parks

City of Austin Pools and Splash Pads

The Contemporary Austin at Laguna Gloria

Crowe's Nest Farm

THE GOURDEN

Dart Bowl

Deep Eddy Pool

Dinosaur Park

Dougherty Arts Theater

Downtown Farmers' Market

Ella Wooten Pool at Mueller

Emma Long Metropolitan Park

George Washington Carver Museum and Cultural Center

Hamilton Pool Preserve

Hideout Theatre—Flying Theater Machine Group

Irving and Hazeline Smith Trail

Kiddie Acres

Krause Springs

Lady Bird Johnson Wildflower Center

Long Center

Lou Neff Point in Zilker Park

Mayfield Park and Preserve

McKinney Falls State Park

McKinney Roughs Nature Park

Millennium Youth Entertainment Complex

Mount Bonnell

Mueller Farmers' Market

Mueller Parks and Trails

Pedernales Falls State Park

Peter Pan Mini-Golf

Pioneer Farms

Playland Skate Center

River Place Nature Trail

Round Rock Express

Rowing Dock in Zilker Park

St. Edward's Trail

Scottish Rite Children's Theater

Splash! Exhibit in Zilker Park

Stargazing at the Roughs

Sunset Valley Farmers' and Artisans' Markets

Texas Memorial Museum

Texas Rowing Center in Zilker Park

Texas State Capitol

Thinkery: The New Austin Children's Museum

Tower Garden

Triangle Farmers' Market

Turkey Creek Trail

Umlauf Sculpture Garden in Zilker Park

The Union Underground

University of Texas Tower Tour

Veloway

Walter E. Long Metropolitan Park at Decker Lake

Westcave Outdoor Discovery Center

Westcave Outdoor Discovery Center Star Party

Wild Basin Stargazing and Moonlighting Tours

ZACH Theatre

Zilker Park

Zilker Botanical Gardens

Zilker Nature Preserve and Hiking Trails

Zilker Park Boat Rentals

Zilker Park Playscape

Zilker Zephyr

Tween (ages 10-12)

Annual Events

Austin Dragon Boat Festival

Austin Museum Day

Austin Trail of Lights

Beverly S. Sheffield Zilker Hillside Theatre

Christmas Lights on 37th Street

Chuy's Children Giving to Children Parade

Crowe's Nest Farm Fall Family Fun Fest

Día de Los Muertos Viva La Vida Fest

Eeyore's Birthday Party

Explore UT

Holiday Sing-Along and Downtown Stroll

Ice Skating at Whole Foods

Juggle Fest

Lake Travis Hot Air Balloon Flyover

Luminations at Lady Bird Johnson Wildflower Center

Music Under the Star Concert Series

Muster Days at Camp Mabry

Nature Nights at Lady Bird Johnson Wildflower Center

Rodeo Austin

Shakespeare in the Park

Texas Book Festival

Zilker Holiday Tree

Zilker Kite Festival

Food & Drink

Amy's Ice Creams
Big Top Candy Shop
Casey's New Orleans Snowballs
Central Market
Doc's Backyard
Frank and Angie's Pizzeria
Freddie's Place
Green Mesquite BBQ
Hill's Café
Home Slice Pizza
Matt's El Rancho
P. Terry's Burger Stand
Sno-Beach
Sugar Mama's Bakeshop
Torchy's Tacos

Fun Places to Shop

Austin Books and Comics
BookPeople
Hill Country Galleria
Toy Joy

Outings

Alamo Drafthouse
Austin Duck Adventures
Austin Public Libraries
Austin Steam Train
Austin Zoo
Barton Creek Greenbelt
Barton Springs Pool in Zilker Park
Bat Watching

Blanton Museum of Art
The Bob Bullock Texas State History Museum
Bright Leaf Preserve
Camp Mabry
Capital MetroRail

Capital of Texas Zoo
Capitol Visitors Center
Chaparral Ice Skating
City of Austin Parks
City of Austin Pools and Splash Pads
Dart Bowl
Deep Eddy
Dougherty Arts Theater
Downtown Farmers' Market
Ella Wooten Pool at Mueller
Emma Long Metropolitan Park
George Washington Carver Museum and Cultural Center
Hamilton Pool Preserve
Irving and Hazeline Smith Trail
Krause Springs
Lady Bird Johnson Wildflower Center

Long Center

McKinney Falls State Park

McKinney Roughs Nature Park

Mexic-Arte Museum

Millennium Youth Entertainment Complex

Mount Bonnell

Mueller Parks and Trails

Pedernales Falls State Park

Peter Pan Mini-Golf

Playland Skate Center

River Place Nature Trail

Round Rock Express

Rowing Dock in Zilker Park

St. Edward's Trail

Stargazing at the Roughs

Texas Memorial Museum

Texas Rowing Center in Zilker Park

Texas State Capitol

Turkey Creek Trail

The Union Underground

University of Texas Tower Tour

Veloway

Walter E. Long Metropolitan Park at Decker Lake

Westcave Outdoor Discovery Center

Westcave Outdoor Discovery Center Star Party

Wild Basin Stargazing and Moonlighting Tours

ZACH Theatre

Zilker Nature Preserve and Hiking Trails

Zilker Park Boat Rentals

Listings by Location

North Austin

Alamo Drafthouse

Amy's Ice Creams

Austin Independent School
District Playgrounds

Austin Public Libraries

Austin Steam Train

Capital MetroRail

City of Austin Parks

City of Austin Pools and Splash
Pads

Kiddie Acres

P. Terry's Burger Stand

Phil's Ice House

Pioneer Farms

Round Rock Express Baseball

North Central

Alamo Drafthouse

Amy's Ice Creams

Austin Books and Comics

Austin Independent School
District Playgrounds

Austin Public Libraries

Capital MetroRail

Casey's New Orleans Snowballs

Central Market

Chaparral Ice Skating

City of Austin Parks

City of Austin Pools and Splash
Pads

Dart Bowl

Ella Wooten Pool at Mueller

Mueller Farmers' Market

Mueller Parks and Trails

P. Terry's Burger Stand

Phil's Ice House

Playland Skate Center

Rootin' Ridge

Sno-Beach

Terra Toys

Thinkery: The New Austin
Children's Museum

Triangle Farmers' Market

University of Texas area

Amy's Ice Creams

Blanton Museum of Art

The Bob Bullock Texas State History Museum

City of Austin Parks

City of Austin Pools and Splash Pads

Texas Memorial Museum

Tower Garden

The Union Underground

University of Texas Tower Tour

Downtown

Alamo Drafthouse

Amy's Ice Creams

Ann and Roy Butler Hike and Bike Trail at Lady Bird Lake

Austin Duck Adventures

Austin Public Libraries

Bat Watching

BookPeople

Capital MetroRail

Capitol Visitors Center

Downtown Farmers' Market

Frank and Angie's Pizzeria

Hideout Theatre—Flying Theater Machine Group

Mexic-Arte Museum

Scottish Rite Children's Theater

Texas State Capitol

Toy Joy

Whole Earth Provisions

Whole Foods Rooftop

West Austin

Amy's Ice Creams

Austin Independent School District Playgrounds

Austin Public Libraries

Barton Creek Farmers Market

Barton Creek Greenbelt

Bright Leaf Preserve

Camp Mabry

City of Austin Parks

City of Austin Pools and Splash Pads

The Contemporary Austin at Laguna Gloria

Deep Eddy Pool

Emma Long Metropolitan Park

Irving and Hazeline Smith Trail

Mayfield Park and Preserve

Mount Bonnell

Over the Rainbow

P. Terry's Burger Stand

River Place Nature Trail

St. Edward's Trail

Turkey Creek Trail

Wild Basin Stargazing and
Moonlighting Tours

West of Town

Amy's Ice Creams

Austin Zoo

Hamilton Pool Preserve

Hill Country Galleria Splash Pad

Krause Springs

P. Terry's Burger Stand

Pedernales Falls State Park

Westcave Outdoor Discovery
Center

Westcave Outdoor Discovery
Center Star Party

East Austin

Amy's Ice Creams

Ann and Roy Butler Hike and
Bike Trail at Lady Bird Lake

Austin Independent School
District Playgrounds

Austin Public Libraries

Boggy Creek Farm

Capital MetroRail

City of Austin Parks

City of Austin Pools and Splash
Pads

George Washington Carver
Museum and Cultural Center

Millennium Youth Entertainment
Complex

Walter E. Long Metropolitan
Park at Decker Lake

East of Town

Capital of Texas Zoo

Crowe's Nest Farm

Dinosaur Park

McKinney Falls State Park

McKinney Roughs Nature Park

Stargazing at the Roughs

South Austin

Alamo Drafthouse

Amy's Ice Creams

Anna's Toy Depot

Austin Independent School
District Playgrounds

Austin Public Libraries

Barton Creek Greenbelt

Big Top Candy Shop

Butler Park

City of Austin Parks

City of Austin Pools and Splash
Pads

Doc's Backyard

Dougherty Arts Theater

Eco-Wise

Freddie's Place

Green Mesquite BBQ

Hill's Café

Home Slice Pizza

Lady Bird Johnson Wildflower Center

Long Center

Matt's El Rancho

P. Terry's Burger Stand

Peter Pan Mini-Golf

Phil's Ice House

Sno-Beach

Sugar Mama's Bakeshop

Sunset Valley Farmers' and Artisans' Markets

Torchy's Tacos

Veloway

Whole Earth Provisions

ZACH Theatre

Zilker Park

Ann and Roy Butler Hike and Bike Trail at Lady Bird Lake

Austin Nature and Science Center

Barton Creek Greenbelt

Barton Springs Pool

Lou Neff Point

Rowing Dock

Splash! Exhibit

Texas Rowing Center

Umlauf Sculpture Garden

Zilker Botanical Gardens

Zilker Nature Preserve and Hiking Trails

Zilker Park Boat Rentals

Zilker Park Playscape

Zilker Zephyr

Free Activities and Events

Free Places

Ann and Roy Butler Hike and Bike Trail at Lady Bird Lake

Austin Independent School District Playgrounds

Austin Public Libraries

Barton Creek Farmers Market

Barton Creek Greenbelt

Bat Watching

Boggy Creek Farm

Bright Leaf Preserve

Butler Park

Camp Mabry

Capitol Visitors Center

City of Austin Parks

City of Austin Neighborhood Pools and Splash Pads

The Contemporary Austin at Laguna Gloria grounds

Downtown Farmers' Market

George Washington Carver Museum and Cultural Center

Hill Country Galleria Splash Pad

Irving and Hazeline Smith Trail

Mayfield Park and Preserve

Mount Bonnell

Mueller Farmers' Market

Mueller Parks and Trails

River Place Nature Trail

St. Edward's Trail

Stargazing at the Roughs

Sunset Valley Farmers' and Artisans' Markets

Texas Memorial Museum

Texas State Capitol

Tower Garden

Triangle Farmers' Market

Turkey Creek Trail

Veloway

Zilker Park

    Austin Nature and Science Center

    Lou Neff Point

    Splash! Exhibit

    Zilker Nature Preserve and Hiking Trails

    Zilker Park Playscape

Occasionally Free

Alamo Drafthouse: Alamo Kids' Club on last Saturdays

Alamo Kids' Camp each summer

Blanton Museum of Art: Free admission Thursdays

Bob Bullock Texas State History Museum: First Sundays noon–6PM

The Contemporary Austin at Laguna Gloria: Free admission Tuesdays

Lady Bird Johnson Wildflower Center: Free admission in January

Long Center: Free Fun Family Events

Mexic-Arte Museum: Free admission Sundays

Thinkery: The New Austin Children's Museum: Wednesdays 5–8PM Sundays 5–6PM

Free Annual Events

Austin Dragon Boat Festival

Austin Museum Day

Austin Trail of Lights

Beverly S. Sheffield Zilker Hillside Theatre

Christmas Lights on 37th Street

Chuy's Children Giving to Children Parade

Día de Los Muertos Viva La Vida Fest

Eeyore's Birthday Party

Explore UT

Holiday Sing-Along and Downtown Stroll

Lake Travis Hot Air Balloon Flyover

Luminations at Lady Bird Johnson Wildflower Center

Music Under the Star Concert Series

Muster Days at Camp Mabry

Nature Nights at Lady Bird Wildflower Center

Shakespeare in the Park

Texas Book Festival

Zilker Holiday Tree

Zilker Kite Festival

Places to Go

The city's best local, outdoorsy, cultural and "weird" family-friendly places

Alamo Drafthouse

Be warned: watching a movie at the Alamo Drafthouse will spoil you and make any other movie theater pale in comparison. In addition to popcorn (with real melted butter) and bottomless sodas, the theater boasts a full menu ranging from classic cheese pizzas on the kids' menu to grilled eggplant and jalapeño pizzas or prosciutto and goat cheeseburgers on the adult menu. Wine, beer, and dessert selections are also available. While movie candy is always an option, so are adult milkshakes, root beer floats, or freshly baked cookies.

Place your order on cards that servers sneak by to collect. Then you can dine at the table in front of you and watch the show. Arrive early for the short films and animated classics dug up from the archives, always an interesting treat related to the theme of the movie you're about to see. (Parents, the Alamo Drafthouse's signature events are also perfect for date nights, from Mystery Science Theater-style live comedy and quote-alongs to dinner and drink specials uniquely paired with the featured film.)

With plenty of expertise and attitude, the Alamo Drafthouse takes the movie experience seriously. So texting, talking, or children under six (except during kid events and weekly Baby Days) are not allowed. That said, they also have quite a bit of fun with the whole movie-going affair and cater to young crowds during special events such as these:

Baby Days at the Alamo — Infants and their parents are welcome on Baby Days each Tuesday for all shows before 2PM (with the exception of the Ritz location). The sound in the theaters is slightly lowered, and many infants find the darkness of the theater a good place to sleep. If they do fuss a bit, you'll find yourself among a tolerant crowd, and no one will kick them out. Free for babies.

Alamo Kids' Club — On the last Saturday of every month in the fall and spring, the Alamo Drafthouse hosts a free special screening of a children's classic. Check the website or call for time, age limits, and location.

Alamo Kids' Camp — The Alamo hosts several free movies at locations around town during school breaks and the hot summer months. The online calendar lists showings, times, and locations.

LOCATION & PHONE

North

Lakeline
14028 N US Hwy. 183, Bldg. F
(512) 476-1320

North Central

The Village
2700 W. Anderson Ln.
(512) 476-1320

Downtown

The Ritz
320 E. 6th St.
(512) 476-1320

South

South Lamar
1120 S. Lamar Blvd.
(512) 476-1320

Slaughter Lane
5701 W. Slaughter Ln.
(512) 476-1320

WEBSITE www.drafthouse.com/austin

Amy's Ice Creams

 I scream, you scream, we all scream for ICE CREAM! Amy's is especially worth screaming about for several reasons:

For one, it's yummy! Old standbys like Belgian Chocolate, Dark Chocolate, Mexican Vanilla, and Sweet Cream are scooped up alongside a rotating selection of creative flavors like Oatmeal Raisin Cookie, S'mores, Mint Ice Cream Sandwich, Cheesecake, Strawberry Lime Pie, or Peanut Butter Honey Sandwich. And forget "toppings." At Amy's you choose from a long list of "crush'ns" that are chopped, crushed, and mixed into your slab of ice cream by hand to create a flavor of your own delicious devising. (There are fruit ices, yogurts, milkshakes, and smoothies too.)

Two, it's an experience. Amy's hires wacky, fun-loving staff. So don't be surprised if you are handed an empty bowl and asked to take a few steps back to catch your ice cream as it is tossed to you across the room. (Don't worry—they're good sports. If you miss, they'll make you another one.)

And three, it's local. Amy opened her first shop on 35th Street and Guadalupe in 1984 and shops have been popping up all over town (and Texas) ever since.

If you want to make your trip to Amy's even more of an experience, visit the Arboretum location where you can wander down a short path to play on giant marble cows beneath the trees. Or continue on to take a trail down to the pond to feed the geese and ducks.

Three other fun locations are paired with *Phil's Icehouse* that makes great burgers and serves local draft beer. These not only have cows to play on but playscapes so kids can burn off sugar highs. With ice cream as dessert, you can make an afternoon or evening of it.

LOCATION, PHONE, AND HOURS

North

Arboretum
10000 Research Blvd., Ste. 140
(512) 345-1006
Sunday – Thursday
11:30AM – midnight
Friday – Saturday
11:30AM – 1AM

Amy's Ice Creams & Phil's Icehouse
13265 N. Hwy 183
(512) 918-2697
Sunday – Thursday
11AM – 10PM
Friday – Saturday
11AM – 11PM

North Central

Amy's Ice Creams & Phil's Icehouse
5624 Burnet Rd.
(512) 538-2697
Sunday – Thursday
11AM – 10:30PM
Friday – Saturday
11AM – 11:30PM

University of Texas Area

Guadalupe
3500 Guadalupe St.
(512) 458-6895
Sunday – Thursday
11:30AM – midnight
Friday – Saturday
11:30AM – 1AM

Downtown

6th and Lamar
1012 W. 6th St.
(512) 480-0673
Sunday – Thursday
11AM – midnight
Friday – Saturday
11AM – 1AM

West

Mira Vista
2805 Bee Caves Rd. #416
(512) 328-2697
Sunday – Thursday
11AM – 10:30PM
Friday – Saturday
11AM – 11:30PM

West of Austin

Hill Country Galleria
13420 Galleria Cir.
(512) 263-2903
Sunday – Thursday
11:30AM – 10PM
Friday – Saturday
11:30AM – 11PM

East

AIBA Airport
(512) 530-2918
Sunday – Friday
9AM – 8PM
Saturday
11AM – 6PM

South

SoCo
1301 S. Congress Ave.
(512) 440-7488
Sunday – Thursday
11:30AM – 11PM
Friday – Saturday
11:30AM – midnight

Amy's Ice Creams
& Phil's Icehouse
2901 S. Lamar Blvd.
(512) 447-2697
Sunday – Thursday
11AM – 11PM
Friday – Saturday
11AM – midnight

Super South
3100 S. Congress Ave. #3A
(512) 851-2697
Sunday – Thursday
11:30AM – 11PM
Friday – Saturday
11:30AM – midnight

The Grove
9600 S. IH-35, Bldg. C, Ste. 400
(512) 282-2697
Sunday – Thursday
11:30AM – 10PM
Friday – Saturday
11:30AM – 11PM

Westgate
4477 S. Lamar Blvd. #790
(512) 891-0573
Sunday – Thursday
11:30AM – 11PM
Friday – Saturday
11:30AM – midnight

WEBSITE www.amysicecreams.com

Ann and Roy Butler Hike and Bike Trail at Lady Bird Lake

This highly popular trail among joggers, bikers, and walkers runs 10 miles through the heart of the city along Lady Bird Lake. It's a beautiful trail and the crushed gravel path makes it a good one for jogging strollers. Especially ideal for parents wanting to get out and exercise is the 4-mile loop from the Mopac bridge to South First Street. Depending on how long your little one is content in a stroller, this stretch can be easily turned into shorter or longer loops (see trail map). If you'd like to take things a bit slower and just enjoy time outdoors together, head to *Lou Neff Point* to feed the ducks. Pack a snack for yourselves too and rest at the gazebo with a nice view of downtown Austin across the lake.

There are plenty of opportunities to diverge from the trail for short excursions (see *Butler Park*, *Zilker Zephyr*, and *Zilker Playscape*). Canoeing and kayaking are other popular activities along the trail (see *Zilker Park Boat Rentals* and *Texas Rowing Center*).

Water stations can be found at the Mopac Expressway and South First Street bridges. Restrooms are available near the parking lot at Auditorium Shores and on the north side of the trail along Cesar Chavez Street.

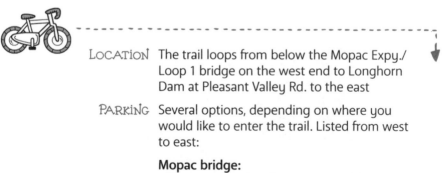

LOCATION The trail loops from below the Mopac Expy./ Loop 1 bridge on the west end to Longhorn Dam at Pleasant Valley Rd. to the east

PARKING Several options, depending on where you would like to enter the trail. Listed from west to east:

Mopac bridge:
A large unpaved parking lot sits beneath the Mopac Expy./Loop 1 bridge at Stratford Dr.

Austin High School:
Street parking and an unpaved lot can be found along the stretch of trail in front of Austin High School (1715 W. Cesar Chavez St.).

Zilker Park:
The parking lot at 2000 Lou Neff Dr. lies just above the trail. Or enter across the street at 2100 Barton Springs Rd. and park near the Zilker Playscape. Stairs leading down to Barton Creek will put you on the trail. (Note that a $5 parking fee is charged in Zilker Park on weekends and holidays from March through Labor Day.)

Riverside Drive near Auditorium Shores:
Street parking and a few small lots are available along W. Riverside Dr. (between S. 1st St. and Lamar Blvd.)

Fiesta Gardens:
Parking lots are available along Festival Beach to the east of I-35 at 2101 Bergman St.

WEBSITE www.austinparks.org/apfweb/park.php?parkId=350

TRAIL MAP www.thetrailfoundation.org/explore/butler-trail-maps

ADMISSION Free

Anna's Toy Depot

Though not big, Anna's Toy Depot sells a constantly rotating selection of used and new toys and is one of those fun shops for both kids and adults. Upon entering, sections of the store pull children like magnets—to dolls and vintage Barbies with handmade clothing, shelves of assorted trucks and cars, craft supplies, musical instruments, LEGO building blocks, dress up clothes for Vikings, cowboys, kings and queens, and bins full of wooden trains and tracks. Parents are drawn to their childhood favorites too—old school Fisher-Price schoolhouses, airplanes and parking garages, Lite-Brites, and Playskool Weebles—toys that bring back the same excitement and wonder that children experience when they step into a toy store.

Locally-owned, Anna's has been in business for over twenty years in south Austin selling the types of toys that last. She favors the plain and simple ones that keep children's attention and encourage imagination, movement, and learning through play. So expect to find more imagination-powered toys than battery-powered and plenty of puzzles, board games, dolls, play sets, sand toys, books, action figures, building sets, and wooden toys of all kinds.

LOCATION	2620 S. Lamar Blvd.
WEBSITE	www.annastoydepot.com
PHONE	(512) 447-8697
HOURS	Monday – Friday 10AM – 6PM
	Saturday 10AM – 5PM

Austin Books and Comics

Knowledgeable employees, staff recommendations, and a section dedicated to carefully selected children's books, graphic novels, and comics make this niche bookstore worth a trip. Parents will recognize classics from their youth shelved alongside a range of currently popular titles. This is also the place to go for superhero t-shirts, lunch boxes, or action figures. (Beware of the giant Incredible Hulk who guards the back of the shop.)

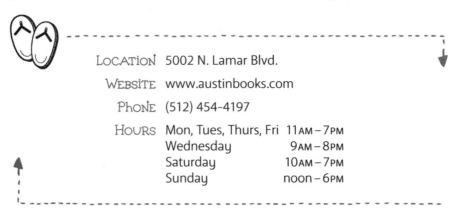

LOCATION   5002 N. Lamar Blvd.

WEBSITE   www.austinbooks.com

PHONE   (512) 454-4197

HOURS   Mon, Tues, Thurs, Fri   11AM – 7PM
            Wednesday   9AM – 8PM
            Saturday   10AM – 7PM
            Sunday   noon – 6PM

Austin Duck Adventures

Visitors will enjoy this open-air tour of the city in an amphibious vehicle that travels from downtown *into* Lake Austin. Locals will likely learn some new nuggets of information as well. For instance, did you know that **Deep Eddy** is the oldest public pool in the state of Texas, and that City Hall was built in the shape of an armadillo? The tour covers  historic downtown buildings, the Capitol and Governor's Mansion, then heads west down Sixth Street to Lake Austin Boulevard. Children are kept busy quacking with souvenir duckbills and waving to passersby while anticipating the big *splash* into Lake Austin where they get an up-close view of the Tom Miller dam. The entire tour lasts approximately one hour and fifteen minutes. Drinks are allowed on board and restrooms are available at the Austin Visitor Center, the pick-up and drop-off point for the duck boat. Reservations are recommended.

LOCATION Tours begin from the Austin Visitor Center located at 209 E. 6th St.

PARKING Curbside meter parking is available downtown, as well as several parking lots and garages. See www.downtownaustin.com/transportation/parking.

WEBSITE www.austinducks.com

PHONE (512) 477-5274

HOURS To ensure your reservation, arrive fifteen to thirty minutes early.

Summer hours (June 1 – Labor Day):

Monday – Friday	11AM, 2PM
Saturday	10AM, noon, 2PM, 4PM
Sunday	11AM, 2PM, 4PM

Regular hours:

Monday – Tuesday	2PM
Wednesday – Friday	11AM, 2PM
Saturday – Sunday	11AM, 2PM, 4PM

ADMISSION

Free	children 2 and under
$15.95	children ages 3-12
$25.95	adults
$23.95	seniors and students

Online reservations are preferred.
Tickets are also sold in the Visitor Center or
over the phone. Prices do not include tax.

Austin Independent School District Playgrounds

There is a healthy supply of playgrounds for young ones in Austin. In addition to those in neighborhood parks (see *City of Austin Parks*), the local school district's playscapes and outdoor facilities are open to the public after school and on weekends and holidays. The Facility Locations Map on the Austin Independent School District website can help identify those closest to you from the nearly one hundred preschool and elementary schools in the district.

LOCATION Throughout the city

WEBSITE www.austinisd.org/schools

PHONE (512) 414-0372

HOURS Playgrounds are available after school and on weekends when not in use by students.

ADMISSION Free

Austin Public Libraries

 The public libraries house several great children's sections in twenty branches around town. They are a great resource for board books, storybooks, reference and activity books, young adult titles, audio books, children's music, and DVDs. They also offer a variety of youth events that grow with children, from storytimes for babies, toddlers, and preschoolers, to those for all ages. Spanish storytimes and pajama times can also be found on the calendar along with puppet shows, LEGO labs, family movie nights, and young adult book clubs.

LOCATION, PHONE, AND HOURS

North

Milwood Branch
12500 Amherst Dr.
(512) 974-9880

Spicewood Springs Branch
8637 Spicewood Springs Rd.
(512) 974-3800

Little Walnut Creek Branch
835 W. Rundberg Ln.
(512) 974-9860

North Village Branch
2505 Steck Ave.
(512) 974-9960

St. John Branch
7500 Blessing Ave.
(512) 974-7570

University Hills Branch
4721 Loyola Ln.
(512) 974-9940

Windsor Park Branch
5833 Westminster Dr.
(512) 974-9840

Yarborough Branch
2200 Hancock Dr.
(512) 974-8820

Downtown

Faulk Central Library
800 Guadalupe St.
(512) 974-7400

West

Howson Branch
2500 Exposition Blvd.
(512) 974-8800

Old Quarry Branch
7051 Village Center Dr.
(512) 974-8860

East . . . .

Carver Branch
1161 Angelina St.
(512) 974-1010

Cepeda Branch
651 N. Pleasant Valley Rd.
(512) 974-7372

Ruiz Branch
1600 Grove Blvd.
(512) 974-7500

Terrazas Branch
1105 E. Cesar Chavez St.
(512) 974-3625

Willie Mae Kirk Branch
3101 Oak Springs Dr.
(512) 974-9920

South . . . .

Hampton Branch at Oak Hill
5125 Convict Hill Rd.
(512) 974-9900

Manchaca Road Branch
5500 Manchaca Rd.
(512) 974-8700

Pleasant Hill Branch
211 E. William Cannon Dr.
(512) 974-3940

Southeast Branch
5803 Nuckols Crossing Rd.
(512) 974-8840

Twin Oaks Branch
1800 S. 5th St.
(512) 974-9980

WEBSITE library.austintexas.gov
library.austintexas.gov/youth-events

PHONE (512) 974-7400

HOURS Hours vary. Some libraries are closed on
Thursdays, Fridays, and/or Sundays. The
following link allows users to find branch
locations, a listing of libraries open today, and
an interactive map: library.austintexas.gov/
locations.

ADMISSION Free

Austin Steam Train

 The Austin Steam Train Association re-opened passenger rail service between Cedar Park and Burnet in 1992 with its Hill Country Flyer. This scenic route to the small town of Burnet continues today with a two-hour layover for lunch on the town square and a Wild West gunfight. Passengers ride in restored cars from the early to mid-1900s. Adding to the authenticity of the experience, volunteers dressed in period clothing with a genuine enthusiasm for the rails serve as conductors, service crew, engineers, and brakemen.

In addition, shorter excursions to the historic 1912 Bertram depot and special event rides have been added to the regular schedule. Crowds of preschoolers flock to "Day Out with Thomas" when Thomas the Tank Engine visits Burnet for thirty-minute rides through the countryside followed by all day *Thomas and Friends*-themed activities and entertainment. The North Pole Flyer is another popular children's event with cookies, hot cocoa, Christmas carols, and a visit from Santa and Mrs. Claus. Other themed rides throughout the year include dinner or lunch on the train.

Ticket reservations are recommended and can be made for open-air cars, climate-controlled or first-class coaches, or lounge cars with private compartments and party rooms. Bring snacks and drinks, or visit the concession car for refreshments.

LOCATION 401 E. Whitestone Blvd., Ste. A-103, Cedar Park

WEB www.austinsteamtrain.org

PHONE (512) 477-8468

HOURS See online schedule or call the ticket office.

ADMISSION Tickets range from $10 and up depending on the event, car class, and age. Children under 3 are free if sitting in an adult's lap. Reservations are recommended; unreserved tickets are sold at the depot ninety minutes before the train departs.

Austin Zoo

The Austin Zoo and Animal Sanctuary is not your typical zoo. It is home to rescue animals ranging from pot-bellied pigs and free-ranging peacocks and roosters to lions, tigers, and bears. Visitors wander along looping dirt trails in the Texas Hill Country to find fox, deer, and longhorn in their natural habitats alongside a range of exotic animals that also make their home here. Children can feed deer, goats, sheep, and llamas in the Petting Zoo. The Rawhide Rocket train offers a fun, quick excursion through ranch land with

nice views for the adults as kids watch out for aliens, flying saucers, and pirate ships along the route! Pack a lunch to eat at one of the many picnic tables on the grounds.

LOCATION 10808 Rawhide Trl.
The Zoo is located off of Hwy. 290 W. approximately 25 miles from downtown Austin and 2½ miles from the "Y" at Oak Hill. To get there, take I-35 or Mopac Expy./Loop 1 to Hwy. 290 W. Turn right at the stoplight at Circle Dr. Follow it for 1½ miles. Turn right on Rawhide Trl. and follow the signs to the zoo.

WEBSITE www.austinzoo.org

PHONE (512) 288-1490

HOURS **Regular hours** (February 1 – October 31):
Daily, 9:30AM – 6PM

Winter hours (November 1 – January 31):
Daily, 9:30AM – 5:30PM

ADMISSION $6 children ages 2-12
$9 adults
$8 students, seniors, military

Barton Creek Farmers Market

One of the most extensive of the markets in town, this one is popular among Austinites for its festive scene and wide range of goodies. It also boasts a nice skyline view. Live music adds to the atmosphere every Saturday as crowds browse the diverse selection of handmade crafts, locally grown fruits and veggies, organic meats, seafood, artisan breads, jellies, and yummy desserts. There is plenty for children to do too with face painting and balloon-making booths and a petting zoo. Check the website for upcoming events plus a detailed list of vendors and available goods.

LOCATION 2901 S. Capital of Texas Hwy.
The market is held in the parking lot of Barton Creek Mall, located at the intersection of S. Mopac Expy./Loop 1 and Capital of Texas Hwy./Loop 360.

WEBSITE www.bartoncreekfarmersmarket.org

PHONE Weekdays (512) 443-0143
Saturdays (512) 280-1976

HOURS Saturday, 9AM–1PM

Barton Creek Greenbelt

This scenic 8-mile trail runs smack dab through the heart of Austin, though you'd never know it from the lush surroundings that follow Barton Creek upstream and make one feel far from city life. The trail begins in **Zilker Park** (just west of Barton Springs Pool) and ends in a secluded neighborhood to the northwest off of Highway 360. There  are several access points to the trail, and most hike it in parts. The best sections for young hikers are detailed below (listed in order from trail's beginning to end).

Zilker Access, *2100 Barton Springs Road in Zilker Park*
This trailhead in Zilker Park marks the beginning of the Barton Creek Greenbelt and can be found at the end of the parking lot near Barton Springs Pool. The first part of this dirt and stone trail stretches through flat, open meadowland and gradually gets greener, shadier, and closer to the water after the first ¼ mile. It's a beautiful section of the trail with several access points to the creek.

Parking: Zilker parking lot near Barton Springs Pool and the Hillside Theater.

Barton Hills Access, *2010 Homedale Drive*
This wooded neighborhood trail leads to The Flats (on the opposite side of the creek from the Zilker access point). Here, Barton Creek flows at the base of tall cliffs and over large limestone slabs. Stay to the right at the split in the trail and it's a ten-minute hike to the creek. One short section down limestone steps might be a tad steep for toddlers and slippery after a rain, but for the most part, the trail is wide, flat, shady, and very scenic. Walking beneath tall trees, you'll cross a small wooden bridge where water trickles down to Barton Creek at the trail's end. Here children can play along the rocks and in the water. When the creek is low, you can cross to the other side to access the rest of the Greenbelt.

Parking: On-street parking along Homedale Drive that runs beside Barton Hills Elementary School.

Spyglass Access, *1601 Spyglass Drive*

This entry point heads straight down a steep, but short, hill of loose rocks to put hikers 1 mile in from the Zilker Park trailhead and within ¼ mile of two swimming areas. You'll pass one of the few restrooms on the trail (a compost toilet). At the bottom of the hill and to the left, it's a very short walk on level ground to The Flats, and just a bit farther to Campbell's Hole. Both are nice spots for playing in the creek, where water flows over limestone, forming small waterfalls and pools.

Parking: Curbside.

360 Access, *3755-B Capitol of Texas Highway*

Best when the creek is flowing and you want to take a dip in it, take this section of the trail down and to the right for a ½-mile trek to Three Falls. After crossing a small wooden bridge and the 3¼ mile marker (from Zilker Park), start listening for the sound of flowing water. A short hike across the creek wash leads to a gorgeous area where the water flows over rock to form a series of small waterfalls and crystal clear pools. Shady areas lie along the bank beneath limestone overhangs. Wear water shoes and swimsuits.

Parking: You'll find a clearly marked access sign at the north end of the office park's lot that backs up to the Greenbelt.

Gaines Creek/Twin Falls Access, *3918 South Mopac Expressway/Loop 1*

This leg of the trail contains two of the Greenbelt's most popular swimming holes, Twin Falls and Sculpture Falls. The trail begins along the top of a ridge and descends to Barton Creek. The hike to Twin Falls is just under ½ mile and while the dirt and stone path might be challenging for young children, what awaits them at the bottom of the trail makes it worth it. The terrain changes to lush creek-side vegetation and water spills over limestone outcroppings to form gorgeous pools. When

the water is up, there are some great jumping-in points, as well as plenty of shallow inlets for wading in the creek. If you're up for an additional 1 ¼-mile hike, Sculpture Falls is another beautiful swimming hole down the trail that tends to be less crowded. Bring your swimsuits.

Parking: From Highway 360, take the frontage road to South Mopac Expressway/Loop 1. Parking is available on the right near the trailhead. This trail gets crowded on spring and summer weekends, so go early.

Trail's End, *1710 Camp Craft Road*

For older children with long legs and some endurance, this steep hill of loose rock and occasional concrete slab steps, fittingly named "The Hill of Life," takes hikers down nearly 300 feet in the first ⅓ mile to surprisingly gorgeous meadowland with a waterfall spilling over the dam into Barton Creek. This trail marks the end of the Greenbelt trail. From here, Sculpture Falls is a 1 ¼-mile hike downstream. The most difficult part of this trail is going back up!

Parking: Curbside in the Lost Hills neighborhood.

WEBSITE www.austinparks.org/our-parks
Search the park database for "Barton Creek Greenbelt." Choose the access point on the map for information and photographs.

PHONE (512) 974-1250

HOURS Daily, 5AM–10PM

ADMISSION Free

Bat Watching

Beneath the Congress Avenue Bridge live 750,000 female Mexican free-tail bats that stream from the bridge at dusk, traveling 10 to 40 miles across the Hill Country over the course of the night, to hunt. From March through October, crowds of spectators gather in the half-hour before sunset to watch them emerge from their homes in the bridge's crevices. Their numbers double to one and a half million by mid-July when babies are born, making it the largest urban bat colony in North America. The most spectacular time to see them is in August when the pups leave the nursery to hunt bugs with their mothers.

Kids with bedtimes late enough to watch these animals wake up can join the crowds of spectators on the Congress Avenue Bridge, peer up at them from a grassy area along the shore, or follow them by boat. The Bat Hotline at (512) 327-9721 reports expected flight times. Be sure to allow enough time to get a good viewing spot. To learn more about bats, check out the educational kiosks below the bridge or reserve seats on a fun, informative bat watching boat tour.

By land

After 6 PM, parking is free in the Austin American Statesman lot at 305 South Congress Avenue (just south of the bridge, at the intersection of Congress Avenue and Barton Springs Road). After parking, bring a blanket and set up at the Bat Observation Center alongside the lake or head up the stairs onto the bridge and watch from the sidewalk as bats head off in clouds to the east.

Admission: Free

By boat

The companies listed below offer bat watching tours with commentary, making it an educational and fun field trip for the family where tourists and locals will learn some interesting facts about the city and its bat population. Bring snacks and a cooler with drinks and enjoy an evening ride on the lake. Tours last about one hour and leave thirty minutes before sunset. Reservations and early arrival are recommended. The boats are docked just below the Hyatt on Barton Springs Road. Paid parking is available in the hotel lot.

Capital Cruises

PHONE   (512) 480-9264

WEBSITE   www.capitalcruises.com

ADMISSION Free children under 3
           $5   children ages 3-12
           $10   adults
           $8   seniors

Lonestar Riverboat

PHONE   (512) 327-1388

WEBSITE   www.lonestarriverboat.com

ADMISSION Free children under 3
           $7   children ages 3–12
           $10   adults
           $8   seniors

Big Top Candy Shop

Step into this narrow slip of a store, seemingly miles long to children as their eyes pop at the ceiling-to-floor candy selections, and the phrase "like a kid in a candy shop" is taken to a whole new level. The choices of familiar treats, unheard of delectables, and sweets from decades past seem endless: huge lollipops, Payday bars, 5th Avenue, Oh Henry,

candy by the piece, fine chocolates, chocolate covered insects, hard candy, salty candy, bulk candy, gummy anything you can imagine, truffles, licorice, bins of jelly beans, jaw breakers, bubblegum, and Wonka bars. They have it all, including an old-fashioned soda fountain where soda jerks whip up milkshakes, malts, and sodas. Curiosity and delight abound for children and adults alike as they wander the length of this circus-themed shop to peruse candy bins beneath brightly colored posters that feature acts like "Snake Boy" and "Voodoo Witch" alongside brass instruments and steampunk art. It's a museum of goodness.

LOCATION 1706 S. Congress Ave.

PARKING Curbside along Congress Ave. and neighboring streets, or the parking garage behind Guerro's Restaurant at Congress Ave. and Elizabeth St.

WEBSITE www.bigtopcandyshop.tumblr.com

PHONE (512) 462-2220

HOURS **"Open 'til they close," roughly:**
Sunday – Thursday   11AM – 7PM
Friday   11AM – 8PM
Saturday   10AM – 9PM

Blanton Museum of Art

For children used to more interactive museums, the "Please don't touch" rule of the Blanton is a hard one to follow as they pass sleek Grecian sculptures that look smooth to the touch, tempting blobs of paint calling to be smooshed, and large installations seemingly waiting to be rearranged. But if you can get past this urge, or have a young babe in a sling or stroller, there is plenty to take in visually and it's an excellent way to introduce kids to great art. The interior of the building itself is impressive, with its tall, bright white walls and large box-like rooms filled with fascinating treasures and interest-grabbing imagery and color.  Permanent exhibits include American and Contemporary Art, European paintings, Latin American Art, and a Prints and Drawing Gallery. Check the calendar for rotating exhibits and public events. One exhibit that is bound to enchant children is Cildo Meireles' *How to Build Cathedrals* in the Modern Art Gallery. A square pool filled with shining pennies radiates from behind transparent black curtains like a hoard of gold, illuminating the dark room and calling children to come in and touch. And in this room, they can.

LOCATION 200 E. Martin Luther King Jr. Blvd. (on the University of Texas campus at the intersection of Congress Ave. and MLK Blvd.)

PARKING Metered street parking is available in the blocks across MLK Blvd. in addition to several parking garages. The Brazos Garage (at Brazos St. and MLK Blvd.) and Trinity Garage (at Trinity St. and MLK Blvd.) offer reduced rates for museum patrons. Have your ticket validated at the museum. The Bob Bullock Museum's parking garage (across the street at 18th St. and Congress Ave.) is another option.

WEBSITE www.blantonmuseum.org

PHONE Main number (512) 471-7324
Front desk (512) 471-5482

HOURS Tuesday–Friday 10AM–5PM
Saturday 11AM–5PM
Sunday 1PM–5PM
Monday closed

Third Thursdays, the museum is open until 9PM

ADMISSION Free children ages 12 and under
$5 youth ages 13–21
$9 adults
$7 seniors (65+)

Thursdays are free to the public

Bob Bullock Texas State History Museum

As visitors pass the thirty-five-foot bronze star at the museum entrance, they get a clear sense that "everything *is* bigger in Texas." The Bob Bullock houses three floors of exhibit space, an IMAX theatre, a special effects theater, a café, and a gift shop. For students of Texas history, the museum is a must-see. Yet all ages will enjoy the experience, from history-loving parents and grandparents to young patrons interested in Native Americans, cowboys, revolutionary heroes, and astronauts.

A Hall of Special Exhibitions is located on the first floor. The permanent exhibits progress chronologically from the ground level up, beginning with the life of Early Settlers where you'll find log cabins, life-size historical figures, and a tipi theater. Take the stairs up to the Texas Revolution and Statehood on the next floor. The third story showcases Texas farming, ranching, and oil as well as the state's roles in World War II and the space program (where children can get an up-close view of a trainer aircraft and astronaut).

The theaters are also worth a visit. The IMAX Theater shows both educational and current feature-length films. The Texas Spirit Theater features two twenty-five-minute presentations, one on Texas weather and another on the state's history. The latter is fun for its engaging special effects from lightning and fog to rattlesnakes under your seat!

Free monthly family programs are offered too. TEXploration Family Story Times are held on the first

Sunday of each month (when admission to the museum is free). See the online schedule for monthly themes and additional special events.

On Friday evenings in July, the museum hosts a free family summer event (see ***Music Under the Stars*** in the Annual Festivals and Events section).

LOCATION 1800 N. Congress Ave. (at the intersection of Martin Luther King, Jr. Blvd.)

PARKING Museum parking garage (at the corner of 18th St. and Congress Ave.) or curbside meter parking along the streets.

WEBSITE www.TheStoryofTexas.com

PHONE Main number (512) 936-8746
Tickets   (512) 936-4649

HOURS Monday – Saturday 9AM – 6PM
Sunday   noon – 6PM

ADMISSION **Exhibits:**
Free children ages 3 and under
$8   children ages 4-17
$12   adults
$10   seniors and military
Free First Sundays

Tickets for the Texas Spirit Theater and IMAX Theatre and are sold separately, ranging in price from $4 – 12.

Boggy Creek Farm

Boggy Creek Farm sits on five acres with one of Austin's oldest homes used as the farmhouse, hearkening back to a time when farmers fed their neighbors and rooted communities. This sense of community is felt on market days as chefs from Austin's finest restaurants shop alongside neighbors and scores of toddlers. Children are naturally drawn to this farm with its coop full of chickens, a dirt pile filled with old dump trucks and shovels, and room to roam. Here, they learn early on how food moves from field to market to tummies. The market stand

is always filled with fresh-picked veggies, eggs, coffee, goat milk ice cream, and other natural goodies. Despite its close proximity to downtown, a trip to Boggy Creek feels more like being invited over to someone's farmhouse and asked to stay awhile.

LOCATION 3414 Lyons Rd.

WEBSITE www.boggycreekfarm.com

PHONE (512) 926-4650

HOURS Wednesday 8AM–1PM
Saturday 8AM–1PM

BookPeople

Taking up half of the second floor of Texas' largest independent bookstore, BookKids houses one of the biggest collections of children's books in the state, and kids love it! Little ones race up the stairs to walls of board books, storybooks, toys, games, and activity books. Kids can find a cozy reading spot at the built-in amphitheater, or in the secret tunnel built beneath it for crawling through or curling up with a good book. Young adult readers can head to the nearby chapter book section and plop down in comfy

beanbag chairs to peruse titles. Staff recommendations, classics, and award winners are prominently featured, so it is never hard to find a good read.

BookKids strongly supports its readers of all ages, so check the Event Calendar for author visits and book signings, literacy summer camps, and book clubs. For young tots, storytimes are held several mornings a week. Titles and hours can be found in the online calendar. (Get there early for a good seat, as these are popular.)

LOCATION   603 N. Lamar Blvd.

WEBSITE   www.BookPeople.com

PHONE   (512) 472-5050

HOURS   Daily, 9AM–11PM

Bright Leaf Preserve

This two hundred-acre preserve nestled in the northwest hills above Lake Austin is accessible by guided hikes only. Monthly tours are offered the second Saturday and Sunday of each month and last two and a half hours. Older children may enjoy the 4-mile hike that leads across Dry Creek and gradually ascends along a wooded trail of Ashe juniper and native vegetation to the former home of Georgia B. Lucas, the preserve's donor. The house sits atop a hill with a view of the lake and the Pennybacker Bridge in the distance. From here, the hike continues downhill with pretty overlooks to the west and a scenic view of the creek below. Along the tour, guides point out geologic features, fossils, signs of animal life, native and invasive plants, birds (including the endangered golden-cheeked warbler who makes its home here in the spring), and history dating back to the dinosaurs. Wear sturdy shoes and bring a water bottle for this hike.

Younger hikers might enjoy a shorter trek through the preserve. Call or email ahead to request a thirty-minute or one-hour guided tour that stays nearer the creek, or to request a hike on another day or at a different time. With advanced notice, guides can be very accommodating for all ages, interests, and group sizes. Another good time to visit with young ones is during spring and fall special events when short tours are offered. Check the calendar online for dates.

A portable restroom is available near the parking lot. Note that pets are not allowed in the preserve.

LOCATION 4200 Old Bull Creek Rd.

WEBSITE www.brightleaf.org

PHONE (512) 459-7269

EMAIL FriendsOfBrightLeaf@gmail.com

Hours   Tours begin at 9AM on the second Saturday
        and second Sunday of each month except for
        advanced arrangements or special events.

Admission   Free

Butler Park

This park became popular for the Liz Carpenter Fountain, which kids quickly recognized as a giant splash pad. Set within a large circular splash area, its programmed, lighted fountains bubble and shoot water in unexpected patterns, providing kids a fun way to cool off as parents set up watch on towels in nearby grassy areas beneath the trees. Restrooms and drinking fountains are located near the parking lot alongside the Dougherty Arts Center.

While this is one of Austin's favorite splash pads, there is plenty of room to roam at Butler Park as well. A nearby pond provides good fish- and turtle-viewing. Or kids can take the short, twisting trail that circles up Doug Sahm Hill. There they will find a Texas-sized map to traverse by foot and a scenic view of Lady Bird Lake and downtown Austin.

LOCATION 1000 Barton Springs Rd. (in the space between the Palmer Events Center and the Dougherty Arts Center)

PARKING From Barton Springs Rd., turn north into the Dougherty Arts parking lot at the stoplight at Dawson Rd. Another option is to park in the available parking spaces along the stretch of Riverside Dr. between S. 1st St. and Lamar Blvd.

WEBSITE www.austinparks.org/apfweb/park.php?parkId=684

HOURS Monday noon–9:45PM
Tuesday–Sunday 8AM–9:45PM

ADMISSION Free

Camp Mabry

Camp Mabry, an operating military post open to the public, offers a surprising range of activities for young civilians, from tank and aircraft displays to a military museum and even fishing. Extending over eight hundred acres, there is much to explore.

Texas Military Forces Museum

The Texas Military Forces Museum on the grounds houses a large display of exhibits in the former dining hall that will awe visitors, especially young ones. The exhibits span Texas' military history from early settlement to modern day. Kids can enter chuck wagons, greet soldiers on horseback, or check out the army tanks, radio communication shelters, helicopters, and airplanes. In adjoining rooms, impressive dioramas of battles from the Texas Revolution can be found. Visitors can try on soldier uniforms and view military gear and historical artifacts too.

Military Vehicle and Aircraft Displays

Just outside the museum visitors can walk down Armour Row to see an impressive array of army tanks and missile launchers. Cross the street where kids can get an up-close view of the airplanes, helicopters, and artillery displays that circle the jogging track. Visitors are also welcome in the All Faith Chapel on the corner.

Pond and Nature Trail

Bring your own bait for catch-and-release fishing in Camp Mabry's pond. To obtain an annual permit ($5 for adults), stop by the Garrison Command Building just south of the Museum and Armour Row during the weekdays. The pond sits at the

bottom of the hill behind these buildings. It's a bit swampy, but there are small inlets and a bench or two along the bank for fishing (watch for snakes in the late spring and summer). If you take a right onto the dirt road near the pond, you can head upstream to the dam. Scenic and shady, you'll find a small spot along the bank here where you might drop a line. Picnic tables, restrooms, and a short Nature Trail are located in this area.

Muster Days

Each April, Camp Mabry hosts Muster Days, a family-friendly, week-end-long celebration in honor of our military with live music, reenactments, and air shows (see *Muster Days at Camp Mabry* under Annual Festivals and Events).

LOCATION	2210 W. 35th St. The public entrance to Camp Mabry is on 35th St., just west of Mopac Expy./Loop 1. Drive 6/10th of a mile past the old main gate (now barricaded). Go through the light at Exposition Blvd. At the bottom of the hill, just before a flashing traffic signal, turn right onto Maintenance Dr. to the gated entrance. Be sure to bring a photo ID with you, as all visitors must pass through the checkpoint at the gate.
PARKING	For easiest access to the exhibits, park at the Texas Military Forces Museum.
WEBSITE	www.texasmilitaryforcesmuseum.org
PHONE	(512) 782-5659
HOURS	**Museum** Tuesday – Sunday 10AM – 4PM **Grounds** Open to the public during daylight hours
ADMISSION	Free, museum donations are accepted

Capital MetroRail

 Ticket machines, train horns, railroad crossings, engineers, giant windows, and the gentle wobble and whir of the train cars are sure to delight young passengers as they weave through parts of town never seen by car. Locals accustomed to Austin traffic will also be amazed by how quickly they can be transported south to the heart of downtown, or north from neighborhood backyards, through fields and ranch land, into the Texas Hill Country. With only nine stops along the rail's entire stretch from Leander to the Austin Convention Center, one of the nice things about this outing is how easy it is to catch a train. The online schedule is simple to read, tickets are available from a ticket machine at each station, and the rail sticks to its schedule. Keep in mind that trains run most frequently during morning and afternoon commute times. For those who are headed to a particular destination and not simply out for a joy ride, rail connector buses can be taken from most stations. Check the website for parking, schedule, and fares. No food or drink is allowed except in spill-proof containers.

WEBSITE www.capmetro.org/MetroRail

PHONE Main number   (512) 389-7400
Route information (512) 474-1200

HOURS Trains run from approximately 6AM – 7:30PM

FARES Children under 6 ride free

Children ages 6 – 18 ride at a reduced rate
(half the adult price)

Adult fares range from $1 – $2.75 depending
on distance traveled, or you can buy a day
pass for $5.50. Check website for exact fares.
Train tickets work for rail connector buses too.

Capital of Texas Zoo

The Capital of Texas Zoo is located down country roads on ranchland just east of Austin. From behind the office where visitors check in, dirt paths lead past a wide variety of species from zebras, snakes, camels, and monkeys to peacocks, goats, boars, and tigers. There are also a surprising number of endangered and exotic animals on site, a passion of the zookeeper. Children can get close to the pens to greet the animals and learn more about the different species from educational signs posted at each. Especially popular among children are the Prairie Dog Town, Python House, Fruit Bat Colony, and the largest Corral of Guinea Pigs you're likely to see around these parts. If your group is inclined to stay for a picnic, tables can be found in a shaded area near the restrooms.

LOCATION 376A Jenkins Rd., Cedar Creek

WEBSITE www.capitaloftexaszoo.org

PHONE (512) 303-6675

HOURS **Summer hours:**
Daily   9AM – 5PM
Winter hours:
Weekdays 10AM – 4PM
Weekends 10AM – 5PM

ADMISSION Free   children under 2
$7.49 children ages 2-11
$9.99 children ages 12 and up and adults

Capitol Visitors Center

Originally the Texas General Land Office, pristinely restored, this three-story white building located on the edge of the Capitol grounds houses several interactive, hands-on exhibits as well as a tourist information desk and gift shop. It's a great place for kids (and adults) to learn about Texas history.

Upon entering, begin your tour with a quick left into the O. Henry Room to pick up old-timey telephones and listen to the life of the famous short story writer who also worked as a draftsman in the building. The fun, twisting staircase just outside this room leads to the second floor with several exhibit spaces and short film showings. In the main room, children can test their Texas knowledge at one of the star-shaped computer kiosks, dress like a cowboy or cowgirl to learn about the role of ranching in the state's history, and explore the construction of the Capitol building. A favorite among young visitors is The Hero's Reward exhibit. Here, kids can walk through a covered wagon and learn about Texas' road from a republic to statehood, peer through telescopes to get a closer glimpse of the Goddess of Liberty atop the

Capitol building, and visit recreated scenes of early settler life.

Tours are self-guided with docents on hand to answer questions. Large groups can also arrange guided field trips. While you're there, be sure to pack a picnic to enjoy on the Capitol lawn.

LOCATION	112 E. 11th St. (on the southeast end of the Capitol grounds)
PARKING	Two hours of free public parking are available at the Visitor Parking Garage (barring any special events). Enter from either 12th or 13th Sts. between San Jacinto Blvd. and Trinity St. Meter parking is also available along surrounding streets.
WEBSITE	www.tspb.state.tx.us/CVC/home/home.html
PHONE	(512) 305-8400
HOURS	Monday–Saturday 9AM–5PM Sunday noon–5PM
ADMISSION	Free

Casey's New Orleans Snowballs

This family-run business from New Orleans operates out of a little white house with orders placed through the front porch windows. Friendly staff scoop up the softest, fluffiest ice, then use a straw to punch tunnels in it for the hand-mixed syrups to fully saturate the snowball. This extra ice is often flicked on the heads of eagerly awaiting young ones hoping for it to "snow!" These treats come in a range of sizes, from junior flattop to jumbo. In addition to traditional flavors made in-house with pure cane sugar, Casey's also offers sugar-free syrups, juice balls made of 100 % fruit juice, special toppings, and cream flavors that melt in your mouth. The porch can get a bit crowded at times and seating on chairs beneath the shade tree is limited, but most tailgate it from the parking area directly behind the house or cool off with their snowballs on the porch steps, too preoccupied to care where they devour these treats.

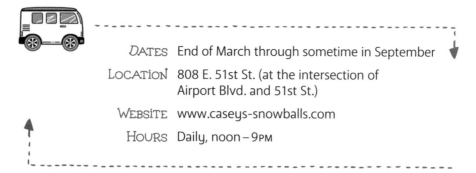

DATES   End of March through sometime in September

LOCATION   808 E. 51st St. (at the intersection of Airport Blvd. and 51st St.)

WEBSITE   www.caseys-snowballs.com

HOURS   Daily, noon – 9PM

Central Market—North Lamar location

This cafe is popular among families for its shady playscape beneath large oak trees and ample outdoor seating that extends from the cafe to the back deck patio near the playground. The restaurant dishes up good, healthy food, tasty drinks, and gelato for dessert. On weekend evenings, early live music sets play out on the patio during dinnertime, with plenty of dancing room. The cafe can get crowded on nice days and evenings, but Central Park (directly behind it) offers additional open space for picnicking, running off energy, feeding ducks, climbing trees, or wandering the ¾-mile trail that loops around the pond. Check the online calendar for special events and free live music (typically performed Thursday through Saturday).

LOCATION 4001 N. Lamar Blvd.

WEBSITE www.centralmarket.com/Stores/Austin-Central.aspx

PHONE (512) 206-1000

CAFE HOURS Sunday – Thursday 7AM – 9PM
Friday – Saturday 7AM – 10PM

Chaparral Ice Skating

Chaparral Ice is the place to go for ice skating, ice hockey, figure skating, or other ice-related sports for all ages. Introductory classes are offered on Saturdays (kids 6 and over can register for a free one), in addition to leagues, summer camps, and birthday party packages. During public skate hours, observers can watch the gracefulness of experienced skaters surrounded by the wide smiles of novices thrilled by the experience, despite their shakiness on the ice. Vending machines are available if your crew works up an appetite. Be sure to dress warm—it's chilly in there!

LOCATION 2525 W. Anderson Ln. at Northcross Mall

WEBSITE www.chaparralice.com

PHONE (512) 252-8500

HOURS Call or check the online calendar for the public skating schedule

ADMISSION $5 Admission and skate rental for children 5 and under

$6 Admission for adults and children over 5

$4 Skate rental for adults and children over 5

City of Austin Parks

The City of Austin maintains over 250 parks, ranging from small outdoor spaces to thousand-acre tracts of parkland. From the Austin Parks Foundation website, you can search by park name for photos and a quick overview of each park's facilities. For an alphabetical listing of all parks and trails, try the Austin Parks and Recreation website. A playground map is also available, as well as an interactive mapping feature that shows park locations and allows users to search for specific facilities — from covered picnic pavilions and swings to playscapes and skate parks.

While each neighborhood recreational area has its own draw, here are some of the city's larger ones:

North

➤ Beverly S. Sheffield Northwest District Park at 7000 Ardath Street

➤ Walnut Creek Metropolitan Park at 12138 North Lamar Boulevard

South

➤ Little Stacy Park at 1400 Alameda Drive that stretches to Big Stacy Park at 700 E. Live Oak Street

➤ Dick Nichols District Park at 8011 Beckett Road

East

➤ Davis White Northeast District Park at 5909 Crystalbrook Drive

➤ Roy G. Guerrero Colorado River Metropolitan Park at 400 Grove Blvd.

For the crown jewel of the Austin park system, see the *Zilker Park* section of this guidebook.

LOCATION	Throughout the city
WEBSITE	www.austinparks.org
INTERACTIVE WEBSITE	www.austintexas.gov/department/parks-and-recreation
PHONE	(512) 974-6700
HOURS	Daily, 5AM–10PM unless otherwise noted
ADMISSION	Free, **with the exception** of entrance fees at Emma Long Metropolitan Park and Walter E. Long Metropolitan Park

City of Austin Pools and Splash Pads

The city of Austin maintains nearly fifty wading pools, splash pads, municipal pools, and neighborhood pools, so you don't have to look far to cool off on sizzling summer days. Swim lessons are offered at several locations. Many facilities have dedicated lap swimming hours or lanes too. The city website lists pools and splash pads by location and type and includes pool schedules. For more detailed descriptions of two of Austin's coolest spring-fed pools, see entries for **Barton Springs Pool** and **Deep Eddy Pool**.

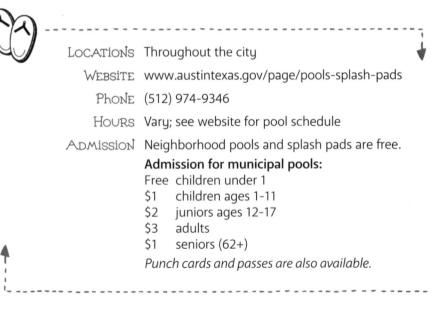

LOCATIONS Throughout the city

WEBSITE www.austintexas.gov/page/pools-splash-pads

PHONE (512) 974-9346

HOURS Vary; see website for pool schedule

ADMISSION Neighborhood pools and splash pads are free.
Admission for municipal pools:
Free children under 1
$1 children ages 1-11
$2 juniors ages 12-17
$3 adults
$1 seniors (62+)
Punch cards and passes are also available.

The Contemporary Austin at Laguna Gloria

The lush twelve-acre grounds of Laguna Gloria are home to the historic Driscoll Villa and sculpture garden and serve as the outdoor complement to the Contemporary Austin's Jones Center downtown. Stone-lined paths present a scenic place for wandering along the shores of Lake Austin, with beautiful structures and art pieces cropping up in unexpected places. The outdoor venue has a distinctly European feel to it, from the 1916 Mediterranean-style villa that sits amidst carefully designed gardens to the Italian fountains and statues. Sharing the grounds with Laguna Gloria is The Art School, where you'll also find some fun art pieces and might happen upon a

visiting peacock from the neighboring Mayfield Preserve.

Each month, Laguna Gloria hosts its "Second Saturdays" event to engage families in creating and experiencing art together (recommended for ages 2–11). Projects relate to the current exhibitions and have included kite making, instrument crafting, yoga, puppet shows, and live musical performances. The Art School also offers art classes year round as well as summer day camps.

LOCATION   3809 W. 35th St.

WEBSITE   www.thecontemporaryaustin.org

PHONE   (512) 458-8191

HOURS   **Grounds**
Monday – Saturday   9AM – 5PM
Sunday   10AM – 5PM

Villa
Tuesday – Sunday   10AM – 4PM
Monday   closed

GALLERY ADMISSION   Free   children under 18 and military
$5   adults
$3   seniors and students
$10   per family for Second Saturdays

Free admission on Tuesdays

Crowe's Nest Farm

Crowe's Nest is an educational working farm in Manor, a half-hour drive from Austin. Throughout the year bus loads of school groups come for field trips, and individual families are welcome to join the tours or visit on special family days. Group tours begin in the big red barn and then branch out on the surrounding paths that lead to cleverly planted children's gardens, milk cow demonstrations in the Dairy Barn, several varieties of chickens in the Hen House, and all kinds of animals, from the types one would expect on a farm—pigs, sheep, goats—to less typical residents like porcupines, emus, and llamas. For the fairy-lovers in your group, a trip to Faeriewood is in order. Pass by the butterfly house and through a magical tunnel of flower-filled vines to an enchanted forest filled with fairies. Visitors can also take a tractor-pulled hayride to learn about the ostriches and bison in the fields. And a large picnic area offers a shady spot to have lunch.

Daily Tours

The farm is open fall and spring for school tours. Individual families are welcome to join. Call ahead for tour times and reservations.

Special Events

In addition to weekday tours, each October the farm opens its doors to the general public for its annual Fall Family Fun Fest with food, music, crafts, and special demonstrations such as sheep shearing, corn shucking, and apple cider making. Weekend family tours are offered in November for Fall Family Fun Days, or visit during the Crowe's Nest Christmas in the Country event when the farm lights up with a living Nativity scene, homemade goods, and down home fun on the farm.

LOCATION	10300 Taylor Ln., Manor
WEBSITE	www.crowesnestfarm.org
PHONE	(512) 272-4418
HOURS & ADMISSION	Call for tour/event times and admission prices. Reservations are required for family weekend tours.

Dart Bowl

Rolling since 1970 and recently remodeled, Dart Bowl is a thirty-two-lane, family-friendly bowling alley. Bumpers are available for young children, and two small arcade areas with video games, billiards, air hockey, and a Laser Maze can be found near the lanes. Snacks and drinks are available from vending machines or from the Dart Bowl  Steakhouse that features a full bar. The restaurant serves up breakfast, Mexican food, burgers, and sandwiches. (The homemade enchiladas are a favorite among regulars.) Near the entryway, kids will enjoy looking through the glass cases filled with an interesting collection of bowling memorabilia, a tribute to the sport. Before you come, be sure to check the website for coupons and specials.

LOCATION 5700 Grover Ave.
(directly behind McCallum High School)

WEBSITE www.dartbowl.com

PHONE (512) 452-2518

HOURS Sunday – Thursday 9AM – 11PM
Friday – Saturday 9AM – 1:30AM

RATES $3.25 Monday – Friday before 6PM
(per person/per game)

$3.85 Monday – Friday after 6PM, weekends,
holidays (per person/per game)

$3.00 Shoe rental (per pair/all day)

Deep Eddy Pool

The oldest public pool in the state of Texas, its spring-fed waters rival **Barton Springs** in temperature, ranging from 65-75 degrees. It's the place to take young ones on a hot summer day and is a favorite among lap swimmers and families for its clear, non-chlorinated water. A zero-depth wading pool roped off at the 1-foot mark makes it ideal for the youngest swimmers. On the other side of the rope, this shallow end of the pool gradually gets up to 3½ feet, where a concrete wall divides the other end into lap swimming and a deeper recreational swim area. There is plenty of space in the surrounding lawn to set up a towel in the sun or beneath the shade of cottonwoods. Deep Eddy has a designated snack area near the newly renovated, open-air bathhouse. In the summer, check the schedule for Splash Party Movie Nights, one of the few ways to stay cool while catching an outdoor flick in the summer.

Picnic tables and a toddler playscape are also located next door at Eilers Park where you can walk down to a dock for a view of Lady Bird Lake. The trail below the pool connects to the **Ann and Roy Butler Hike and Bike Trail** too (at the Mopac Expressway bridge).

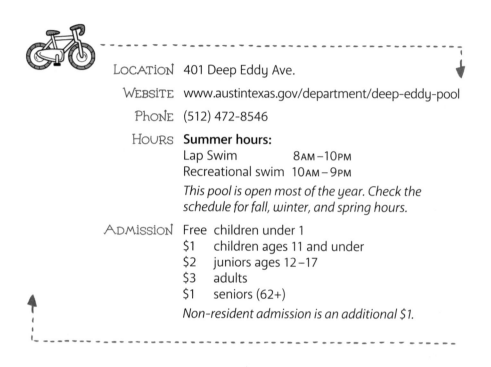

LOCATION 401 Deep Eddy Ave.

WEBSITE www.austintexas.gov/department/deep-eddy-pool

PHONE (512) 472-8546

HOURS **Summer hours:**
Lap Swim   8AM–10PM
Recreational swim 10AM–9PM

This pool is open most of the year. Check the schedule for fall, winter, and spring hours.

ADMISSION Free children under 1
$1   children ages 11 and under
$2   juniors ages 12–17
$3   adults
$1   seniors (62+)

Non-resident admission is an additional $1.

Dinosaur Park

Walk this nature trail and watch out for dinosaurs! The unique park features impressive, life-size, painted dinosaur figures strategically placed along a wooded gravel pathway to give children a feel for what the world must have been like when dinosaurs roamed. All ages will enjoy the scavenger hunt to search for cleverly hidden remnants from prehistoric times interspersed with the main exhibits. Young children can follow the clue numbers painted on dinosaur footprints while older children can then read the clues and help in the hunt. Educational plaques offer additional scientific facts about each exhibit. The trail is self-guided and takes about half an hour. The loop begins at the edge of a playground and picnic area and circles back to it, where children can enjoy lunch, play on the playscape, or dig for fossils in long sand tables filled with shovels and brushes. For those hooked on dinosaurs by the end, the gift shop sells a variety of dino-themed puzzles, toys, and activities.

LOCATION 893 Union Chapel Rd., Cedar Creek

WEBSITE www.thedinopark.com

PHONE (512) 321-6262

HOURS **Regular hours:**
Saturday – Sunday 10AM – 4PM
Summer hours:
Tuesday – Sunday 10AM – 4PM
Field trips and group tours are available throughout the week. Call for reservations.

ADMISSION Free children under 24 months
$7 children 2 and up and adults

Doc's Backyard

From this restaurant, large garage doors open onto an expansive outdoor picnic area and pavilion that slope to two playscapes, making it a favorite among families. The playground rests beneath a grove of oak trees backed by ranchland that provides a scenic backdrop for watching the kids play. The playground is good for all ages with a separate, smaller corralled area with a playhouse for toddlers. The menu features American fare with some Mexican flair, and a full bar is available with a selection of Texas craft beers. Kids can order staples like mini-burgers, mini-hot dogs, and crustless PB&J sandwiches.

LOCATION 5207 Brodie Ln.

WEBSITE www.eatdrinkdocs.com

PHONE (512) 892-5200

HOURS Daily, 11AM – midnight

Dougherty Arts Theater

 The Dougherty Arts Center is home to an art gallery and art school for all ages as well as a theater that puts on several great productions for young audiences throughout the year. The theater seats 150, making it small enough that children can feel a part of the action, and many of the performances are based on children's classics that are sure to entertain. Call the theater or check online for this year's schedule.

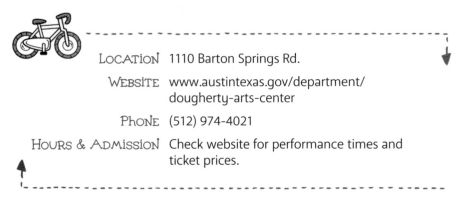

LOCATION 1110 Barton Springs Rd.

WEBSITE www.austintexas.gov/department/dougherty-arts-center

PHONE (512) 974-4021

HOURS & ADMISSION Check website for performance times and ticket prices.

Downtown Farmers' Market

Flowers, veggies, honey, popsicles, jellies, grass-fed beef, dairy products, ethnic foods, and artisan breads give just a taste of what the downtown market offers. Tents line the

entire block at Republic Square Park and offer a large variety of the homegrown. Live music plays. And kids flock to the Sustainable Food Center's "Be Groovy, Be Green" children's tent where face paint and other activities can be found. Check the online calendar for special kid events and activities too.

LOCATION 422 W. Guadalupe St.

PARKING A large lot next door and the City Hall parking garage two blocks south offer free parking during the market. If you arrive early, reduced paid parking can be found in the State Garage on San Antonio St. between 3rd and 4th Sts. Street meter parking is another option.

WEBSITE www.sfcfarmersmarketdowntown.org

HOURS Saturday, 9AM–1PM

Eco-Wise

 This shop specializes in earth-friendly, non-toxic products, including baby items and toys for all ages. Organic clothing, cloth diapers, carriers, wooden toys, and a collection of board books and storybooks fill the baby section. Other children's items are located just as they would be at home: lunchboxes in the kitchen section, child-size gardening tools in the outdoor area, and shelves of earth-friendly toys in the middle of it all. With an emphasis on science and educational toys, it's a treasure trove of cooperative games, puzzles, and classic toys.

LOCATION 110 W. Elizabeth St.

WEBSITE www.ecowise.com

PHONE (512) 326-4474

HOURS Monday–Friday 9:30AM–6:30PM
Saturday   10AM–6PM
Sunday   12PM–5PM

Ella Wooten Pool

This beautiful neighborhood pool for the *Mueller* development opens its gates to non-residents in the afternoons. A great one for young swimmers, the shallow end is a good-sized half circle that ranges in depth from 3 inches to just under 2 feet. Mosaic fish and turtles on the pool's bottom encourage children to get their faces wet for a closer

glimpse. An umbrella-shaded wall divides this end from the big pool,

which starts at 3½-feet and gradually gets deeper towards the lap lanes at the far end. A grassy lawn surrounds the swimming pool, and stone bathhouses can be found at the entrance. A playscape, basketball court, and picnic tables lie just outside the pool gates.

LOCATION 2047 McCloskey St.
(between Pinkney St. and Mendez St.)

WEBSITE www.muelleraustinonline.com/pool.php

NON-RESIDENT HOURS Tuesday – Sunday 1PM – 7PM
Monday closed

ADMISSION $1 children ages 11 and under
$2 juniors ages 12-17
$3 adults
$1 seniors

Emma Long Metropolitan Park

 This park makes you feel as if you've gotten away, while not traveling far at all. Emma Long rests on a long slip of land that borders scenic Lake Austin. A large swimming area with a sandy beach makes for a great, relaxing place to spend the day. Kids can swim, build sandcastles, look for seashells along the shore, jump from the docks, or bob in the waves from passing boaters. So be sure to pack the buckets, shovels, and rafts. A grove of giant oak trees and plenty of waterfront picnic tables and grills sit adjacent to this day use area, and restrooms with showers are just up the hill. The park also has sand volleyball courts, fishing, and boat ramps.

Camping is available on a first come, first served basis. Camping spots in the Bluff area are a bit exposed and close together with the lake in the near distance, while the spots in the Grove and Utility Area lie on the shadier end of the park, half of them waterfront. It's some of the nearest camping to be found within city limits.

LOCATION 1600 City Park Rd.

DIRECTIONS Take FM 2222 west. At the traffic light, turn onto City Park Rd. and follow it to the end (6.2 miles).

WEBSITE www.austintexas.gov/department/city-parks

PHONE (512) 346-1831

HOURS Day use hours are from 7AM–10PM
Park gates are locked from 10PM–7AM

ADMISSION $5 entrance fee per vehicle Monday–Thursday
$10 entrance fee per vehicle Friday–Sunday and holidays
$10 primitive campsite (no water or electricity)
$20 primitive campsite with water only
$20 non-shoreline utility campsite
$25 shoreline utility campsite

Frank and Angie's Pizzeria

This cozy, Italian-themed restaurant opened its doors in 1995 with family recipes that traveled from Sicily with the owner's grandparents. The kitchen dishes up thin crust pizzas, pasta dishes, and Italian sandwiches, in kid-size portions too. It's casual dining with a family-friendly atmosphere. For antsy toddlers, a shaded outdoor waiting area offers a little open space to roam. Outside seating is available in a screened-in patio nestled in the trees above Shoal Creek.

LOCATION 508 West Ave.

WEBSITE www.hutsfrankandangies.com

PHONE (512) 472-3534

HOURS Monday – Friday 11AM – 10PM
Saturday noon – 10PM
Sunday 5PM – 10PM

Freddie's Place

For a kid-friendly South Austin experience, head to Freddie's, known for its laid-back atmosphere and large outdoor seating area. It's best on nice evenings when you can sit outside beneath the shade of tall trees along Bouldin Creek and enjoy comfort food ranging from fish tacos and burgers to frito pie and chicken fried steak. A playscape is situated in the back corner near the stage where live music plays Thursday-Sunday nights.

LOCATION 1703 S. 1st St.

WEBSITE www.freddiesplaceaustin.com

PHONE (512) 445-9197

HOURS Daily, 7AM–10:30PM

George Washington Carver Museum and Cultural Center

This museum celebrates African American culture and historical achievement through its four galleries: an interactive Juneteenth exhibit, another featuring prominent Central Texas families where visitors can examine their own family trees, a Community Gallery with rotating art exhibits, and the "Let's Pretend, Dr. Carver" Children's Gallery where children can put on a lab coat and examine the many scientific contributions and inventions made by the African American community. In addition to these interactive exhibits, special activities and programs are scheduled for the museum's annual Juneteenth celebration. You can also combine your outing to the Carver Museum with a trip to the Carver Public Library next door or the Kealing playground behind it.

LOCATION 1165 Angelina St.

WEBSITE www.austintexas.gov/department/george-washington-carver-museum-and-cultural-center

PHONE (512) 974-4926

HOURS Monday – Wednesday 10AM – 6PM
Thursday 10AM – 9PM
Friday 10AM – 5PM
Saturday 10AM – 4PM
Sunday closed

ADMISSION Free

Green Mesquite BBQ

"Smokin' the good stuff since 1988," this BBQ venue has the feel of an even older Austin where Texas tradition and the city's relaxed hippie days meet. You can easily disappear into the era as you step in to find small, round barstools at the counter and green and white checkered tablecloths at the booths. Or head outside to the courtyard with its green picnic tables and stage beneath the shade of trees and awning where folks sit and listen to live music on weekends. The menu features BBQ plates, chicken fried steak, burgers, fried catfish, and veggies. Kid plates are available too. Cobbler, pecan pie, or ice cream top it all off.

LOCATION   1400 Barton Springs Rd.

WEBSITE   www.greenmesquite.net

PHONE   (512) 479-0485

HOURS   Daily, 11AM–10PM

*Live music plays Thursdays – Sundays,
typically between 7PM – 9:30PM*

Hamilton Pool Preserve

Just 30 miles west of downtown Austin, Hamilton Pool Preserve draws crowds for its cool water and scenic setting. A two-lane highway of gorgeous meadows and ranchland along Hamilton Pool Road takes you to the preserve, especially popular in the summer months for its swimming hole.

After parking just past the entrance station, you can get to the pool by taking a ¼-mile gravel and stone trail that leads from the cactus, oak, and ashe juniper of the uplands to a creek-lined path of bald cypress, moss, and fern. Cross a small wooden bridge and a few stepping stones to arrive at the base of the grotto where a 50-foot waterfall spills from a large limestone outcropping into the pool. The flow of water depends on recent rains, but the pool level remains relatively constant (and nice and cool). Swimmers can set up towels, chairs, and picnics in the partially shady beach area where the water is shallow. Or take the path that circles the pool to set up camp on large, flat rocks beneath the cave-like rock overhang directly behind the waterfall.

There are two restroom areas located within the park—compost toilets near the parking lot and portable toilets on the trail just before you arrive at the pool.

While most head to the grotto, you can also take a ¾-mile hike from the parking lot to the Pedernales River. Begin on the trail to the pool. Then at the River Trail marker at the base of the hill, go left to follow the creek down to the water.

A few tips before heading to Hamilton Pool with children:

➤ Call ahead.

If you plan on swimming, call for the daily update to make sure the pool is open before driving out. A heavy rain can lead to a spike in bacterial counts or water debris and temporary pool closures.

➤ **Go early!**
Park officials limit the number of vehicles to seventy-five at a time to protect the rare and endangered plants and animals in this part of the Balcones Canyonlands Preserve. Once capacity is reached, admittance is on a "one out, one in" system. On weekends and by mid-day in the summer, waits can get up to two hours. So it's best to go early, especially with kids.

➤ **Pack snacks and drinks.**
Food, drinks (no glass), and ice chests are allowed in the Preserve.

➤ **No pets are allowed.**

LOCATION	24300 Hamilton Pool Rd., Dripping Springs
WEBSITE	www.co.travis.tx.us/tnr/parks/hamilton_pool.asp
PHONE	(512) 264-2740
HOURS	Daily, 9AM – 6PM (no entry after 5:30PM)
ADMISSION	$3 per pedestrian/bike
	$15 per vehicle

Hideout Theatre

This intimate theater hidden above the Hideout Coffeeshop on Congress Avenue makes an engaging space for children to watch, and participate in, theater. The improvisational Flying Theater Group that performs Sunday kid shows invites its audience to help join in the storytelling and acting. With an area front-and-center of the stage specif-  ically for younger folks, it makes for easy recruiting—and quite unexpected storylines! It's great, fun entertainment for children and their parents. Acting classes and summer camps are also offered through the Hideout. (The coffeeshop makes a convenient spot to grab a snack and drinks before or after the show too.)

LOCATION	617 Congress Ave.
PARKING	Curbside meter parking is available downtown, as well as several parking lots and garages: www.downtownaustin.com/transportation/parking
WEBSITE	www.hideouttheatre.com/shows/flyingtheatermachine
PHONE	(512) 443-3688
HOURS	Sunday shows typically at 2PM
ADMISSION	Tickets $7-10

Hill Country Galleria Splash Pad

The gently sloping hillside amphitheater at the Galleria leads to a splash pad for kids and a pergola with shaded tables for their parents. A bookstore, yogurt shop, Whole Foods Market, and children's retailers line the streets nearby and public restrooms are directly across the way. What's more, an **Amy's Ice Creams** sits atop the hill overlooking the splash pad and the Bee Cave Library lies directly behind it. Since this circular splash pad doubles as a stage, call ahead or check the event calendar to make sure the interactive fountains are open before you suit up.

LOCATION	12700 Hill Country Blvd., Bee Cave
WEBSITE	www.hillcountrygalleria.com
PHONE	(512) 263-0001
HOURS	Monday–Saturday 10 AM – 9 PM
	Sunday noon – 6 PM
ADMISSION	Free

Hill's Café

Hill's Cafe hearkens back to Old Austin. Built over fifty years ago by Sam "Posey" Hill and the Goodnight family, it's a large restaurant with long wood bars, wildlife mounted on the walls, and down-home Southern cooking. The Hill's burger has been voted best in Austin and the chicken fried steak, the best in Texas. Families will especially enjoy the large patio out back where you can eat under huge oak trees and live music plays three nights a week. There is ample room for kids to roam and explore the barn-like buildings, porches, and stone structures as they wait for their meals to come.

LOCATION   4700 S. Congress Ave.

WEBSITE   www.hillscafe.com

PHONE   (512) 851-9300

HOURS   Daily, 11AM–10PM

Home Slice Pizza

This classic New York style pizza joint serves delicious thin crust pies, Italian sub sandwiches, calzones, and salads. Slices are available daily until 6:30 in the evening and again after 9:30. The hip restaurant located in the heart of SoCo stays busy! So go early and on a weekday to avoid a long wait, or simply be prepared to order some drinks and hang out. To keep up with demand, the owners also opened a "takeout and slices only" shop next door. So if hungry tummies can't wait, order a pie or grab some slices at More Home Slice.

LOCATIONS	1415 S. Congress Ave. (Home Slice Pizza)
	1421 S. Congress Ave. (More Home Slice)
WEBSITE	www.homeslicepizza.com
PHONE	(512) 444-7437

HOURS FOR HOME SLICE PIZZA		
Mon, Wed, Thurs	11AM–11PM
Friday–Saturday	11AM–midnight
Sunday	noon–11PM
Tuesday	closed

HOURS FOR MORE HOME SLICE		
Monday–Thursday	11AM–11PM
Friday–Saturday	11AM–3AM
Sunday	noon–11PM

Irving and Hazeline Smith Trail

Located just up the road from the more extensive Bull Creek Trail, this hike is perfect for little legs. The 1½-mile loop trail takes hikers along an easy, well-marked, and mostly shaded dirt path. Markers along the way point out the stone wall where a Victory Garden once grew, water-falls, and conservation lessons. The highlight is a side loop  mid-way through that leads to the creek and waterfalls. Because Bull Creek is home to the Jollyville Plateau salamander, the land is protected for water quality, so no swimming, picnics, or dogs are allowed. But the clear water makes turtle spotting easy and a bench provides a good, peaceful resting spot after playing near the creek before trekking back.

LOCATION 5479 Old Spicewood Springs Rd.

PARKING A dirt parking lot lies directly across the road from the trail entrance.

WEBSITE www.austinparks.org/apfweb/park.php?parkId=686

TRAIL MAP www.ci.austin.tx.us/water/wildland/downloads/stenis.pdf

ADMISSION Free

Kiddie Acres

While most amusement parks require kids to measure 48 inches in height to go on rides, this park is ideal for the shorter crowd that doesn't usually make the cut. Open since 1979, Kiddie Acres' charm lies in its unique, vintage carnival rides. A carousel, miniature ferris wheel, and small boats, jeeps, and flying airplanes—with working propellers—spin around at a child's pace. A miniature train circles the grounds and pony rides are offered in the corral. A round of ten tickets will cover all rides, or add 18 holes of miniature golf. Weekdays are calm, with weekends being busiest for birthday party celebrations, but lines are never too long and most of the area is shaded. Picnic tables and benches are available for concessions from the park.

LOCATION   4800 W. Howard Ln.

WEBSITE   www.kiddieacres.com

PHONE   (512) 255-4131

HOURS   **May – October**
Tuesday – Friday 10AM – 6PM
Saturday   10AM – 7PM
Sunday   noon – 6PM

November – April
Tuesday – Friday noon – 6PM
Saturday   noon – 7PM
Sunday   noon – 6PM

TICKET PRICES (+ TAX) $2   single ticket
$18   round (10 tickets)

Miniature golf rates are 3 tickets, or $5.00 per adult and $4.00 per child 12 and under.

Discounts are offered for twenty-five tickets or large groups. Wednesday is discount day ($1.20 per ticket) and Sunday is Grandparents Day ($1.20 for tickets purchased by grandparents).

Krause Springs

Krause Springs is a beautiful swimming hole and campground in Spicewood, about a half hour's drive west of Austin. The water on the property comes from cool natural springs so the water feels *fine*, especially on hot summer days.

Upon nearing the springs, ranchland and dirt road quickly give way to Hill Country oasis where streams run beneath lush vegetation under the shade of cypress trees. You can take a dip in the small but refreshing spring-fed swimming pool. A bathhouse and restrooms are located on either side of the pool with several handcrafted rock and stone picnic tables scattered beneath the cypress. Just beyond this area is a lookout point where water spills down moss-covered limestone cliffs to the swimming hole and creek below. A rather steep set of stairs and a more gradual trail both lead to the springs where limestone rocks provide spots for setting up a towel. Be careful here—the rocks can be slippery.

Bring a cooler and a raft or tube with you too. As swimmers kick back in colorful tubes and kids splash into the water from the rope swing near the picturesque grotto and waterfall, it paints an idyllic scene of summertime in the Hill Country.

If you'd like to stay overnight, primitive tent camping and RV sites are nestled a little farther down the creek under the trees. (No glass or pets are allowed.)

LOCATION 404 Krause Spring Rd., Spicewood

DIRECTIONS From Hwy. 71 W., turn right at the traffic signal in Spicewood onto Spur 191. Take it for half a mile. Then take another right onto County Rd. 404. The gated entrance to Krause Springs will be on your left.

WEBSITE www.krausesprings.net

PHONE (830) 693-4181

HOURS Daily, 9AM – sundown

ADMISSION Free children under 4
$4 children 4–11
$6 children 12 and older and adults

No credit cards accepted

DAILY CAMPING RATES $6 children under 12
$12 adults and children 12 and over
$12 additional fee for water and electric site

Lady Bird Johnson Wildflower Center

Beautiful native landscaping, acres of gardens and trails, and Spanish style architecture make the Wildflower Center a gorgeous place to visit any time of the year. As children make their way up the entrance walk, they will undoubtedly spot the turtles and fish in the wetland pond and the deep, crystal clear pool just ahead in the center of the Courtyard. From here, children can go left to the Little House (through a child-sized door leading into a small schoolroom where nature-related books, puzzles, and art activities are always available) or head to the right to the Visitor's Gallery and Observation Tower. A nice view of the grasslands below rewards those who climb the circling stairs and ramps of the sandstone tower.

The pathways around the grounds lead through woodland gardens, theme gardens, butterfly gardens, an insectary, and the McDermott Learning Center. For those looking for additional hiking, four trails span outwards from the Wildflower Center. The shortest is the Woodland Trail, a shaded ¼-mile hike with a trailhead just below the Tower (between the library and administration building). It will take you to the butterfly garden and carriage house. The longest is the Restoration Research Trail, a 1-mile hike through grasslands. Maps are available online and in the Wildflower Center Store where you check in.

Shaded picnic areas rest at either end of the Center. An inviting café also offers a place to cool off and enjoy snacks, drinks, or lunch while enjoying the view.

The Lady Bird Johnson Wildflower Center hosts several free, family-friendly events each year too. See the Events section for educational **Nature Nights** in the summers and **Luminations** during the holidays. January is also Free Admission month.

LOCATION	4801 La Crosse Ave.
WEBSITE	www.wildflower.org
PHONE	(512) 232-0100
HOURS	Tuesday – Saturday 9AM – 5PM
	Sunday noon – 5PM
	Monday closed
	Open daily with extended hours during Wildflower Days in the spring
ADMISSION	Free children ages 4 and under
	$3 children ages 5-12
	$7 students ages 13 and older
	$9 adults
	$7 seniors (65+)

Long Center

The Long Center is one of Austin's newest performing arts centers, housing a large performance hall, a studio theater, indoor community spaces, and an outdoor terrace and lawn for events, with a beautiful view of downtown from across Lady Bird Lake. The versatility of the Long Center allows for a variety of programming from the likes of Austin Shakespeare, Ballet Austin, Pollyanna Theatre Company, Austin Lyric Opera, and local musicians. Family-friendly performances and special events are scheduled throughout the year. Especially popular is the ALL summer LONG series that offers affordable (and often free) entertainment during the summer months. These fun events have included dances, live music acts, movies on the lawn, trailer food picnics, concerts by the Austin Symphony, and Bubblepalooza! (a fun-filled day of bubbles, food, live music, and children's activities on the terrace).

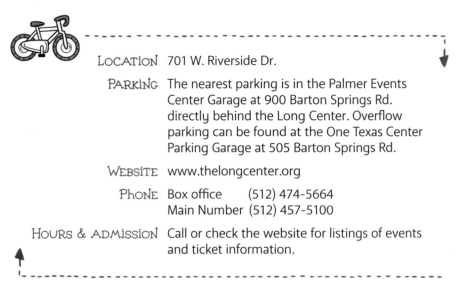

LOCATION 701 W. Riverside Dr.

PARKING The nearest parking is in the Palmer Events Center Garage at 900 Barton Springs Rd. directly behind the Long Center. Overflow parking can be found at the One Texas Center Parking Garage at 505 Barton Springs Rd.

WEBSITE www.thelongcenter.org

PHONE Box office   (512) 474-5664
Main Number (512) 457-5100

HOURS & ADMISSION Call or check the website for listings of events and ticket information.

Matt's El Rancho

With its mission-style architecture, handsomely engraved front doors, and outdoor courtyard, entering Matt's feels like walking into old Mexico. The "King of Mexican Food," Matt Martinez and his family have been in business since 1952 serving Tex-Mex favorites like enchilada plates, carne guisada, tacos, fajitas, and grilled sirloin steaks as well as more traditional Mexican seafood dishes. The children's menu offers a range of options too, from fajitas, grilled veggies on Spanish rice, or broccoli with a side of queso to cheese quesadillas, chicken strips, or burgers. Kids can watch tortilla making and the grill behind large glass windows near the kitchen. The outdoor courtyard also provides a family-friendly place to eat, relaxing for parents and entertaining for kids with its fountain filled with fish.

LOCATION 2613 S. Lamar Blvd.

WEBSITE www.mattselrancho.com

PHONE (512) 462-9333

HOURS Mon, Wed, Thurs, Sun 11AM–10PM
Friday–Saturday 11AM–11PM
Tuesday closed

Mayfield Park and Preserve

Mayfield is a wonderful place to wander with children. Peacocks roam freely, welcoming visitors to the historic cottage and gardens. Winding rock pathways lead past lily pad-filled ponds, beautiful gardens, old stone structures, and towering palm trees in the expansive courtyard. It offers young visitors a world of discovery.

Beyond the stone wall enclosing the cottage grounds lie picnic tables and over twenty additional acres to explore. The trailhead nearest the cottage takes hikers through easy, wooded trails to Lake Austin, across Taylor Creek, and to the base of limestone cliffs. Another trailhead lies at the west end of the parking lot near the chimney swift tower and portable restrooms. Taken right, it leads towards Laguna Gloria; or go left to connect with the other trails. The hikes are all fairly short. Due to the wildlife in the park and preserve, no pets are allowed.

LOCATION 3505 W. 35th St.

WEBSITE www.austinparks.org/apfweb/park.php?&parkId=283
www.mayfieldpark.org

PHONE (512) 474-9692

HOURS Daily, dawn to dusk

ADMISSION Free

McKinney Falls State Park

This state park is a popular one with creek access, a hike and bike trail, and overnight camping less than half an hour from Austin. With nearly 750 acres to play in, it's perfect for daytrips or weekend camping. Check in at the entrance station to find out about park events, from ranger-led fishing to guided hikes. Park maps are available at the Headquarters and in the Smith Visitors Center where kids can touch animal pelts, create nature crafts, and check out exhibits about the area.

Onion Creek flows through the park, providing wading, fishing, and swimming. At both the Upper and Lower Falls, water spills across limestone slabs to form swimming holes. (Be sure to inquire at the office about the suitability of swimming as bacterial counts can occasionally spike after heavy rains.) Fishing poles are free for the borrowing from the Visitors Center and bait can be purchased at the Headquarters.

A shady stretch with a number of fairly secluded tables along the wooded Onion Creek Hike and Bike Trail make a perfect spot for picnics. The paved 2.8-mile trail provides great biking for all ages too (with just a couple of steep hills). Older children might enjoy the new 1-mile mountain bike trail or the isolated Homestead Trail, accessible by crossing the Lower Falls.

For hiking, stop in the Smith Visitors Center to pick up a guide map to the nearby Rock Shelter Interpretive Trail, an easy ¾-mile hike above the creek. The lush, shaded first half of the loop leads past large cypress trees, across wooden bridges, and beneath a beautiful, large rock shelter that extends over the trail. Little legs may want to turn back here, or continue on (stay to the right) to loop back through more exposed meadowland.

Overnight camping is also available. You can choose from eighty-four water and electric sites clustered beneath trees; eight hike-in, water-only sites along the creek; six shelters; or a youth group area. Call ahead for reservations (for all except hike-in campsites).

LOCATION	5808 McKinney Falls Pkwy.
DIRECTIONS	From Austin, take Hwy 183 S. to McKinney Falls Pkwy.
WEBSITE	www.tpwd.state.tx.us/state-parks/mckinney-falls
PHONE	(512) 243-1643
RESERVATIONS	(512) 389-8900 www.tpwd.state.tx.us/business/park_reservations
HOURS	Daily, 8AM–10PM
ADMISSION	Free children 12 and under $6 teens and adults for day use
CAMPING FEES	$15 walk-in tent sites (100–200 yds.) along Onion Creek (not reserveable) $20 campsites with water & electricity (30 amp) $24 campsites with water & electricity (50 amp) $40 screened shelters

McKinney Roughs Nature Park

McKinney Roughs is a beautiful LCRA Park located between Austin and Bastrop. A short jaunt from the city, it offers 18 miles of hiking trails ranging from rugged Texas Hill Country and bluffs to piney canyons and shady, wooded trails along the Colorado River. It's a great hiking destination with well-maintained trails and grounds.

Check in at the Visitors Center to pick up a park map that lists all trails and their mileages along with suggested hikes and approximate times for completing them. Children will enjoy observing the Center's impressive fish, turtle, snake, and salamander habitats or examining bits of nature at the touching table. Just outside the building, scenic paths loop among educational exhibits. For those with a bit more endurance, hit the hiking trails with water, snacks, sunscreen, and hats packed. Be sure to check the park calendar for fun community and educational programs too. Stargazing, moonlight rafting, GPS adventuring, scavenger hunts, and camps are offered throughout the year.

LOCATION 1884 Hwy. 71 W., Cedar Creek

WEBSITE www.lcra.org/mckinneyroughs

PHONE (512) 303-5073

HOURS Monday – Saturday 8AM – 5PM
Sunday   noon – 5PM
Sunday hiking from Pope Bend Trailhead only

ADMISSION Free children 12 and under
$5 teens and adults
$2 seniors (65+)

Mexic-Arte Museum

Mexic-Arte has been bringing Mexican, Latin American, and Latino art to Austin for over twenty-five years. While the three exhibit spaces are primarily adult-focused, a good time to check out the museum with children is on Family Days. These are held on Sundays throughout the year, and special art activities are offered to engage children in the current exhibit. The museum also hosts ***Viva La Vida Fest*** each fall, a popular annual event to celebrate El Día de los Muertos, or the Day of the Dead (see entry in the Annual Events section).

LOCATION 419 Congress Ave.

WEBSITE www.mexic-artemuseum.org

PHONE (512) 480-9373

HOURS Monday – Thursday 10AM – 6PM
Friday – Saturday 10AM – 5PM
Sunday noon – 5PM

ADMISSION $1 children 12 and under
$5 teens and adults
$4 seniors and students
Free on Sundays

Millennium Youth Entertainment Complex

Upon entering the Millennium, parents of the 80s and 90s will feel as if they've taken a step back in time when weekends were spent skating to Michael Jackson, eating snack bar pizza, and hitting the arcades. Built in 1999, the youth entertainment complex houses a bowling alley, roller skating rink, food court, movie theater, and video arcade. The alley offers sixteen lanes of bowling with side bumpers available for young bowlers and a food court nearby. Skaters of all ages take over the rink, complete with laser  lights, music, and plenty of room to roll. On Saturdays, when things get busy, skating time is limited to two-hour sessions (call ahead for the schedule if you're headed there just to skate). The movie theater plays current, family-friendly films, and the arcade is decent-sized with games ranging from toddler-age merry-go-rounds and auto racing videogames to air hockey and billiards. Owned by the City of Austin and run by a private company, costs are kept at a minimum. Birthday party and group packages are also available.

LOCATION 1156 Hargrave St.

WEBSITE www.myec.net

PHONE (512) 472-6932

HOURS Wednesday – Thursday 10AM – 7PM
Friday – Saturday 10AM – 11PM
Sunday – Tuesday closed

Mount Bonnell

The highlight of this short hike is the impressive view of Lake Austin and the hills from atop Mount Bonnell. For kids excited about stairs, they can climb the long rock stairway to the top, or little legs can take a more gradual route up the gravel path from the far north end of the parking lot. Giant limestone slabs line this end of the trail where hikers can glimpse the Pennybacker Bridge in the distance or watch ski boats speed by below. (Keep an eye on toddlers since the area off of the trail here is rather steep.) A few picnic tables are scattered around the park and short side trails lead to secret, hidden spots among the trees as well as to a scenic view of the Austin skyline at the far south end. No restrooms are on site, but it's a short trek up and back.

LOCATION 3800 Mount Bonnell Rd.

WEBSITE www.austinparks.org/apfweb/park.php?parkId=287

PHONE (512) 477-1566

HOURS Daily, 5AM–10PM

ADMISSION Free

Mueller Farmers' Market

That Mueller has become one of the city's most vibrant farmers' markets comes as no surprise. With families within walking distance and locals coming for the playgrounds, trailer eatery, and hike and bike trail, it posed an organic complement to the neighborhood. The market is housed in the historic Browning Hangar, sandwiched between food trailers on one side and a lake on the other. (Bring bread crumbs to feed the swans.) Children's activities are organized on the lawn in the shade of trees. With live music playing, it's a great place for a picnic. Good eats can be found aplenty in the market stalls—from ethnic, vegan, and gluten-free foods to delicious desserts. Also for  the picking are wines, flowers, preserves, farm-fresh veggies, grass-fed beef, and coffees and teas. If you want to stick around even after vendors close shop, there is plenty to do nearby (see *Muller Parks and Trails*, *Ella Wooten Pool*, or the *Thinkery*).

LOCATION 4550 Mueller Blvd.

WEBSITE www.texasfarmersmarket.org/mueller

PHONE (512) 363-5700

HOURS Sunday, 10AM – 2PM

Mueller Parks and Trails

At Mueller Lake Park, children float through the air on giant, saucer-shaped swings. They climb on rubber, rope, and metal; spin on geometric contraptions; and balance on a rotating beam that serves as a merry-go-round. It's a fun playscape, unique from most in Austin. For young ones, the smaller playscape and sand area that overlook the lake provide a good space to play, so pack the buckets and shovels. Restrooms are located just outside the gate to the enclosed playground area. Picnic tables can be found by the playscapes and scattered along the nearby lake trail, where catch-and-release fishing is a popular activity.

The neighborhood offers a range of activities for families. Just beyond the playground, the paved trail provides a perfect place for children to bike, trike, scooter, or wander around the lake to feed the ducks and geese. Those with more endurance can continue along the decomposed granite trail that winds for 5 miles throughout the Mueller development—past large, metal spider art pieces, waterfalls spilling into ponds, and native grasslands.

Several additional playgrounds and picnic areas are also located nearby. Near the Mueller Retail Center, a beautiful trellised picnic area provides shade within close sight of a playscape. And a square block of parkland with basketball court, playground, picnic areas, and *Ella Wooten Pool* lies in the Southwest section of the neighborhood.

LOCATION 4550 Mueller Blvd.
The Mueller Neighborhood is located on the site of Austin's former Robert Mueller Municipal Airport, along the east side of Airport Blvd.

WEBSITE www.muelleraustin.com/parks-and-open-spaces

Over the Rainbow

In Tarrytown since 1975, this smartly-organized shop specializes in traditional toys for a wide range of ages. Seasonal toys greet one upon entering, books are shelved at one end of the store, boy and girl sections overlap in areas that appeal to both genders (outdoor toys, dress up clothes, science kits, and games), and a baby/toddler area sits along the back wall far from the front door. The bookstore houses an impressive collection of classic board books, award winning picture books, and favorite young adult series. It's one of those rare places where you can turn a child loose to choose a book and know that it will be a good one. The same goes for the toys.

LOCATION	2727 Exposition Blvd.
WEBSITE	www.overtherainbowaustin.com
PHONE	(512) 477-2954
HOURS	Monday – Friday 9:30AM – 5:30PM
	Saturday 9:30AM – 5PM

P. Terry's Burger Stand

 P. Terry's is a modern twist on the classic burger stand. With a simple menu of burgers, fries, and shakes, it's fast but healthier than most fast food. They use all-natural antibiotic-free beef, make their own veggie burger, and fry fresh-cut potatoes in non-hydrogenated oil. Family-friendly, the locations listed below also offer outdoor seating with a sand pile for the kids.

LOCATION AND HOURS

North

Mopac and Parmer
12301 N. Mopac Expy.
(512) 719-4810
Monday – Thursday
7AM – 11PM
Friday
7AM – midnight
Saturday
8AM – midnight
Sunday
8AM – 11PM

North Central

32nd and Lamar
3303 N. Lamar Blvd.
(512) 371-9975
Monday – Thursday
7AM – midnight
Friday
7AM – 1AM
Saturday
8AM – 1AM
Sunday
8AM – midnight

West

Village at Westlake
701 S. Capital of Texas Hwy.,
Bldg. H
(512) 306-0779
Monday – Thursday
7AM – 10PM
Friday
7AM – 11PM
Saturday
8AM – 11PM
Sunday
8AM – 10PM

West of Town

Lake Travis at Turnquist Plaza
3311 RR 620 S.
(512) 263-9433
Sunday – Thursday
11AM – 10PM
Friday – Saturday
11AM – 11PM

South

Barton Springs and S. Lamar
404 S. Lamar Blvd.
(512) 473-2217

Monday – Thursday
7AM – 1AM

Friday
7AM – 3AM

Saturday
8AM – 3AM

Sunday
8AM – 1AM

MoPac and William Cannon
4228 W. William Cannon Dr.
(512) 358-0380

Monday – Friday
7AM – 11PM

Saturday – Sunday
8AM – 11PM

WEBSITE   www.pterrys.com

Pedernales Falls State Park

Though less than an hour's drive from the fast pace of the city, you'll feel as if you have gone much farther when all that can be seen from scenic overlooks are trees and river; deer can be spotted walking just beyond your campground; and unlike many nice hikes in Austin that carry the constant roar of traffic, all that can be heard here is the roar of water after a heavy rain.

Pedernales Falls, one of the most popular destinations in the park, lies on the north end. A short hike on gravel leads to a scenic overlook of the falls, which can be quite impressive depending on recent rains. Water levels vary with the weather, but the beach area tends to be a great place for all ages to hike along the boulders, wade in the river, collect seashells, build sandcastles, or play in spring-fed pools. Keep a lookout for herons and other wildlife drawn to the water.

Another area on this end of the park that bird lovers will enjoy is the Bird Blind. Entering these shelters, visitors can sneak a peek from behind glass windows at an amazing numbers of birds of all kinds flitting about in their native habitats. Labeled photos teach visitors which birds they are seeing so they can contribute to the daily count.

For short, scenic hikes with the kids, head to the campgrounds. The Pedernales Hill Country Nature Trail loops behind campsites #13 and #21 and leads to an overlook with a beautiful view of Twin Falls pool spilling over a cliff into the creek below. Another trail near campsite #33 passes the park amphitheater and is an easy walk down to the river. If the water is low enough, hikers can cross to a long strip of beach area to play. Older children might enjoy the 4 miles of hiking and mountain biking on the other side through Hill Country terrain.

The campgrounds provide nice camping if you decide to stay awhile. A cluster of seventy fairly isolated, good-sized sites are located in the middle of the park surrounded by trees, each with a shaded picnic table and grill. Restrooms and showers are nearby. Call ahead for reservations.

LOCATION	2585 Park Rd. 6026, Johnson City
DIRECTIONS	From Austin, take Hwy. 290 W. through Dripping Springs. Turn right onto FM 3232 and drive 6 miles to the park entrance.
WEBSITE	www.tpwd.state.tx.us/state-parks/pedernales-falls
PHONE	(830) 868-7304
RESERVATIONS	(512) 389-8900 www.tpwd.state.tx.us/business/park_reservations
HOURS	Daily, 8AM–10PM The park occasionally closes for wildlife management activities so call ahead or check the park's website before heading out.
ADMISSION	Free children ages 12 and under $6 teens and adults for day use
CAMPING FEES	$20 camping sites with water and electricity $10 primitive sites (hike-in, 2-mile min.)

Peter Pan Mini-Golf

This local business has been family owned and operated since 1948 and its charm lies in the relaxed atmosphere as golfers putt through the legs of timeless characters like Peter Pan and a giant T-Rex, through the mouth of a whale, or under unique pirates, turtles, and lighthouses. With two 18-hole courses to choose from, the area is small enough that kids can easily do both. The east course is slightly less challenging with fewer uphill holes. It is a bit more maze-like though and golfers have to pay

attention to the number for the next hole (good counting practice for younger kids, and if you get out of order, no one seems to mind). The west side is more clearly laid out with a number of iconic figures. While the course can get a bit hot on sunny afternoons, ice chests are allowed (without glass) and sno-cones are sold at the ticket counter. Or to make it an even more Austinesque day, head east just up the street to the ever-popular *Sno-Beach* on Barton Springs Road.

LOCATION 1207 Barton Springs Rd.

WEBSITE www.peterpanminigolf.com

PHONE (512) 472-1033

HOURS Vary by season; stays open late but call ahead if going early

ADMISSION Cash or check only

One course (18 holes):
$4 children 5 and under
$6 adults and children 6 and over

Both courses (36 holes):
$7 children 5 and under
$9 adults and children 6 and over

Phil's Ice House

This popular family-friendly restaurant serves up tasty burgers (named after funky local neighborhoods), sweet potato fries, and draft beer. A children's menu is also available. The original location on Burnet Road was converted from the old Allandale post office and gas station. On nice days, the garage doors in the dining area open and seating flows out to the picnic tables near the playscape. At the location on South Lamar Boulevard, the outdoor seating and play area sit beneath the shade of big oak trees. The newest Phil's in North Austin also features live feed from its skydiving neighbor, iFLY. To top it all off, these restaurants are connected to *Amy's Ice Creams*, so save room for dessert!

LOCATION, PHONE, AND HOURS

North. . . . .
    13265 US Hwy. 183 N
    (512) 257-8750
    Sunday – Thursday
    11AM – 9PM
    Friday – Saturday
    11AM – 11PM

South. . . . .
    2901 S. Lamar Blvd.
    (512) 707-8704
    Sunday – Thursday
    11AM – 9PM
    Friday – Saturday
    11AM – 11PM

North Central. . . . .
    5620 Burnet Rd.
    (512) 524-1212
    Sunday – Thursday
    11AM – 9PM
    Friday – Saturday
    11AM – 10PM

WEBSITE www.philsicehouse.com

Pioneer Farms

Visitors take a trip back in time to farm life in the mid- to late-1800s as they step onto the grounds of this ninety-acre outdoor museum. (Young fans of the Biscuit Brothers will likely recognize many places as the backdrop for the popular children's television show.) Stop in the General Store to pick up a free Walking Tour brochure to guide you along the ¾-mile path that loops around the farm. Then head out to experience history come alive on a German immigrant homestead, in a wooded Tonkawa Indian Camp, and at an old Settlers' Cabin. You'll pass chickens in the henhouse and cow, pig, and donkeys in the corrals. A working blacksmith shop near the Scarborough Barn holds demonstrations on weekends. Continue on to visit the Cotton Planter's homestead with a kitchen and spinning room out back. There are several good spots for a picnic lunch, and restrooms for Menfolk and Womenfolk can be found throughout the park.

Before leaving, be sure to grab a copy of the *Pioneer Farms Gazette* with news and upcoming events, or check the website. One of the farm's most popular annual events, the **Austin Family Music Festival**, is held here along with camps, special demonstrations, reenactments, and homeschool and scouting days throughout the year.

LOCATION 10621 Pioneer Farms Dr.

WEBSITE www.pioneerfarms.org

PHONE (512) 837-1215

HOURS Friday – Sunday 10AM – 5PM

ADMISSION Pay in the General Store

Free children ages 2 and under
$6   children ages 3 and up
$8   adults

Playland Skate Center

 Playland Skate Center houses Austin's largest skating rink, complete with flashing lights, glittery disco balls, and a range of music. Handrails line the entire rink at a child's level, with plenty of openings for skaters to get on and off to rest on benches against the walls. For those who need some practice before feeling comfortable on the big rink, a small children's skate area is set apart at the rear of the building. Lessons are also available. A small arcade and two-story indoor playscape keep younger, non-skating siblings occupied.

LOCATION 8822 McCann Dr.

WEBSITE www.playlandskatecenter.com

PHONE (512) 452-1901

HOURS & ADMISSION Call or check the website for the public skating schedule and cost of admission.
Admission typically costs $6–$8, including skates.
Playscape Area is $3 for children under 52".

River Place Nature Trail

Found in a hilly subdivision in west Austin, the trail is part of the Balcones Canyonland Preserve. Originally a 3½-mile trail and one of the steepest in the city, sections have been closed to protect the endangered golden-cheeked warbler. The trails that do remain open year round at lower elevations are both scenic and easy enough for young hikers. These are also the best-marked trails around, with maps and a kiosk at every junction.

The best trail for kids begins at the Boardwalk, near a small pond. The short wooden pathway takes hikers along the water's boundary to the dirt path and log steps of Lower Panther Trail, a ½-mile hike through shaded woods along Panther Hollow Creek. Wooden bridges, stepping stones, and surprises at every corner keep children engaged, whether they discover another set of log steps, idyllically-placed benches, turtles in the clear creek, or waterfalls spilling down moss-covered limestone cliffs after rains.

After the first ½ mile, you might turn back where the trail forks (I recommend going out the way you came in; the Water Line Trail is another option, but sunny and less scenic), or decide to continue just a bit farther, up Fern Creek Trail, to a beautiful, clear pool at the base of a small waterfall. A nice wide bench overlooking the pool makes a good spot to look for turtles and rest. Older children may wish to continue the last ½ mile before heading back, but the going does get steeper.

Restrooms with water fountains, a playground, and picnic tables along the creek can be found across the street at Woodlands Park too.

LOCATION 9000 Big View Dr.
(across the street from the soccer fields and playground at Woodlands Park)

PARKING Curbside or in the parking lot at Woodlands Park.

WEBSITE   www.austinexplorer.com/Locations/
ShowLocation.aspx?LocationID=9337

HOURS   Daily, 8AM – sunset

ADMISSION   Free

Rootin' Ridge

This locally-owned toy store has been in business since 1975 and is a treat to visit for its simplicity and charm. Specializing in toys for young children, the small slip of a shop is just their size. Everything in the store is made from wood, much of it hand-crafted onsite. Children can climb a short staircase of wooden steps to a viewing platform to watch toys being drilled, sawed, and sanded smooth. They're the kinds of toys that never lose their appeal, and it's the closest thing to Santa's workshop you are likely to find this side of the North Pole.

LOCATION 1206 W. 38th in the 26 Doors Shopping Center

WEBSITE www.rootinridge.com

PHONE (512) 453-2604

HOURS Monday – Friday 10AM – 5PM
Saturday 10AM – 4PM

Round Rock Express Baseball

Round Rock Express games are an easy family-friendly outing just a short drive from Austin. Minor League baseball fans will love it, but there is plenty for kids to like about going to these games in addition to the sport. For little ones with energy, there is room to roam in the Lawn Seating, or below the Porch section. Be sure to pack a blanket, sunscreen, and baseball hats for "seats" in these areas. The team mascot Spike also wanders through the crowds greeting young fans. And a Fun Zone for kids eight years old and younger contains a playscape, bouncy house, and sport court. Entrance to this area is free, although there is an admission fee for the rock wall and bungee trampolines. Hot dogs, cotton candy, pizza, ice cream, and other baseball fare are available throughout the park. At the end of the games on Sundays, kids are invited to run the bases. Check the schedule for the firework displays too, following the games on Fridays and other select nights.

LOCATION	The Dell Diamond, 3400 E. Palm Valley on Hwy. 79, Round Rock
WEBSITE	www.roundrockexpress.com
PHONE	(512) 255-2255

ADMISSION

Free	children 2 and under
$7	lawn seating
$8	porch seats
$12–14	reserved seating

Prices listed are advance purchase. For tickets at the gate, add $1 to lawn seating and $2 to all other seats. $1 discount for children under 12, military, and seniors (60+).

Several packages are available (see the website or call for info.).

St. Edward's Trail

If you have young children with you, it might be best to approach this 3- to 4-mile loop trail (with several spurs and side shoots) by choosing the type of activity you would like to do rather than trying to complete it all in one trek. With its varied terrain, St. Edward's Trail can easily be viewed as three distinct hikes: through open meadowland (north of the creek), along Bull Creek, and up a wooded path atop the bluffs (south of the creek). There are two main trailheads with a parking lot at each: a smaller one with a sign noting St. Edward's Trail, and a little farther up the road, a larger lot with a kiosk, map, and trailhead.

Meadow Trail

Head right from either trailhead to hike through level, open prairie land grasses and wildflowers. It's an especially pretty hike in the spring. Take a left at any juncture to move from fields to creek.

Creek Trail

St. Edward's Trail is most fun for playing in the creek, especially after a good rain when the water is flowing. The trailhead from the smaller parking lot leads to a shady bank along the water (from the larger parking lot and trailhead, simply head left) where children can wade, race leaves and sticks in the current, or cross on large stepping stones to the bank on the opposite side. Just a bit farther up the trail, an old dam divides the water into pools

and provides scenic views up the creek as well as good turtle and fish spotting. Continue on the trail to a waterfall that spills over bluffs into a limestone pool. From here, you can keep to the trail to eventually loop through the more exposed meadow trail or head back along the creek.

Hill Trail

If you have any hikers in your group with some endurance, they might enjoy crossing the creek (take the trail downstream from the dam to a bank with stepping stones) to the south end of the park that rises above the creek through wooded ashe juniper and oak. It's a scenic trek up the hill as you climb limestone steps and tree roots, with gorgeous views of the creek and fields below. (Young hikers need to pay attention where the trail hugs the edge in places.) While the rise in elevation might become a bit much for little legs, it can be a peaceful and rewarding experience for those who appreciate a steeper rise in elevation than that offered by most trails in the area.

LOCATION 7301 Spicewood Springs Rd.

PARKING There are two parking lots: a small area on the shoulder of the road with a sign for St. Edward's Trail and a larger parking lot with a map and kiosk.

WEBSITE www.austinparks.org/apfweb/park. php?&parkId=339

TRAIL MAP http://www.mountainbiketx.com/downloads/texas/maps/St_Edwards.pdf

PHONE (512) 477-1566

HOURS Daily, 5AM–10PM

ADMISSION Free

Scottish Rite Children's Theater

 Scottish Rite puts on fun children's theater. Most of the productions are adaptations of classic children's tales, made shorter and more interactive for young audiences. The Scottish Rite, formerly a German opera house built in 1871, is home to the oldest operating theater in Austin, seating 250 patrons on the lower level and as many children as will fit on the large carpets front and center of the stage where they can become active participants in the plays. The sets are always impressive and the stories silly and engaging. Afterwards, theater-goers are often invited to meet the cast on stage or in the parlor where they set up with pen and posters to sign autographs.

LOCATION   207 W. 18th St.

WEBSITE   www.scottishritetheater.org

PHONE   (512) 472-5436

HOURS & ADMISSION   Call or check the website for the season's schedule and ticket information.

Sno-Beach

Sno-Beach is one of Austin's most popular sno-cone stands, and one of the city's first food trailers. It has been providing Austinites this summertime staple for over twenty years. The locations are part of the appeal. To cool off inside and out, many combine a trip to the Barton Springs Road location with a plunge in *Barton Springs Pool*. This spot shares an empty lot with a smattering of food trailers. Picnic tables with umbrellas circle the stand. The other location on Guadalupe Street draws University of Texas students and locals from the nearby neighborhoods. Customers line up to choose from a long list of traditional flavors (as

well as a few sugar-free choices), with the option to top it off with caramel or cream. In the face of a changing Austin and due to the transitory nature of food trailers, there's always the chance that Sno-Beach could be on the move, so check the address before you go. But these sweet stands will very likely stick around.

DATES March – October

LOCATIONS **North**
3402 Guadalupe St.
South
801 Barton Springs Rd.

WEBSITE www.snobeachatx.com

HOURS Daily, noon – sundown

Stargazing at the Roughs

McKinney Roughs Nature Park hosts family-friendly stargazing events on Fridays throughout the year. The park opens thirty minutes prior to the program and guests congregate in the parking lot near the Visitors' Center. At sunset, the group travels down a short lantern-lit path to an open gravel lot to observe the night sky. Astronomers identify constellations with a laser pointer and offer visitors a stellar view of the stars, planets, and moon through carefully aimed telescopes. Bring binoculars, refreshments, and chairs. In the case of cloudy or inclement weather, the program may be cancelled so call ahead.

LOCATION 1884 Hwy. 71 W., Cedar Creek

WEBSITE Check the park calendar for dates and event details: www.lcra.org/parks/developed_parks/mckinney_roughs.html

PHONE (512) 303-5073

HOURS 8:30PM–10PM

ADMISSION Free

Sugar Mama's Bakeshop

You have never had cupcakes *this* good: buttery vanilla cupcakes topped with dollops of buttercream frosting and sprinkled with sugar, moist red velvet cupcakes, carrot cupcakes, vegan mint chocolate cupcakes, chocolate cupcakes with chocolate frosting.... This bakery whips up deliciously decadent desserts, made from scratch each morning. Daily specials complement the handful of regular flavors, always with gluten-free or vegan options. Displayed beside the cupcakes are a variety of mini-pies, cookies, and bars to pick from too. The size is good for kids, big and fancy enough to be a special treat without overwhelming their tummies. Grab a seat in the small dining area decked out in 50's retro style to match the names of the cupcakes (from the Marilyn Monroe to the James Brown or Elvis).

LOCATION   1905 S. 1st St.

WEBSITE   www.sugarmamasbakeshop.com

PHONE   (512) 448-3727

HOURS   Tuesday – Saturday 10AM – 8PM
Sunday   11AM – 4PM
Monday   closed

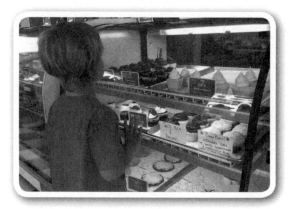

Sunset Valley Farmers' and Artisans' Markets

Despite being located in the Tony Burger Center parking lot, of the farmers' markets in town this one feels most like you're getting out into the country for your veggies. Two markets in one, farmers fill the tree-lined path with their goods while local artisans set up their booths adjacent to beautiful ranchland. An open field at the end of the lot provides children plenty of room to dance while musicians play. Healthy food and drinks are readily available for picnicking.

LOCATION 3200 Jones Rd. outside the Tony Burger Center

WEBSITE www.sfcfarmersmarketsunsetvalley.org

HOURS Saturday, 9AM–1PM

Terra Toys

Terra Toys is a toy store that welcomes play. Children pass by on fire trucks and plasma cars or pushing child-size shopping carts. Gongs, tambourines, and egg shakers sound from the musical instruments section as impromptu bands form. <u>Thomas the Train and Friends</u> clack along wooden tracks on the play table. With ample space for playing and browsing, this independently-owned shop carries a wide range of areas with kid appeal: arts and crafts, scientific exploration, imaginary play, transportation, performance art, games and puzzles, and outdoor activities. Babies have a special area devoted to them, and a fairly extensive collection of storybooks is housed in the rear of the store, along with stuffed animals and puppets. Be prepared to spend more time here than expected.

LOCATION 2438 W. Anderson Ln.

WEBSITE www.terratoys.com

PHONE (512) 445-4489

HOURS Monday – Saturday 9AM – 8PM
Sunday   noon – 6PM

Texas Memorial Museum

This museum will fascinate both children and adults. The trek up a tree-lined slope of steps from the west to this white, fossil-filled fortress, or past dinosaur tracks and a bronze saber-toothed cat from the east marks a passage from this world to one that existed millions of years ago. Upon entering the museum, visitors' attention is immediately arrested by the giant Texas Pterosaur with a forty-foot wingspan that looms overhead. More such exhibits and educational displays fill each of the four floors. Don't miss the Onion Creek Mosasaur in the Hall of Geology and Paleontology that swims among a collection of giant sloths, armadillo ancestors larger than you ever imagined, ancient amphibians, and collections of bones and fossils sure to impress youngsters. The Hall of Texas Wildlife, one floor up, houses more familiar insects and animals from barn owls and rattlesnakes to roadrunners and coyotes. Interactive activities that explore evolution can be found in the Hall of Biodiversity on the top floor.

How many floors you get to and how long you stay at each will depend entirely on your child's interest and age. Regardless of how much you see on a particular visit, it is one of those museums that will contain something novel and interesting each time you go. Be sure to check the museum website for fun, science-oriented events for children hosted throughout the year.

LOCATION	2400 Trinity St. on the University of Texas campus (two blocks north of the UT stadium)
PARKING	San Jacinto Garage next door to the museum at 2401 San Jacinto Blvd.
WEBSITE	www.texasmemorialmuseum.org
PHONE	(512) 471-1604
HOURS	Monday–Thursday 9AM–5PM Friday 9AM–4:45PM Saturday 10AM–4:45PM Sunday 1PM–4:45PM
ADMISSION	Free

Texas State Capitol

The Capitol is a good place for exploring with kids of all ages, from blanket picnics with babies on the lawn, to roaming with toddlers, to leading young ones up the Great Walk lined with cannons and statues of Texas heroes to enter the giant doors of the Capitol. All will be struck by the enormity and grandiosity of the building, but it is also intriguing to see it from a child's perspective where life-sized marble statues and governors' portraits are eyed with wonder, and maze-like hallways of polished granite lead to hidden elevators and secret chambers. Be sure to head to the rotunda to spin under the star in the dome and test the acoustics. Take a peek in the House and Senate chambers. You might also want to visit the underground Capitol Extension where you can grab a snack or meal in the Cafeteria.

Pick up brochures for Self-Guided Tours of the Grounds or the Capitol building or get them online: www.tspb.state.tx.us/spb/plan/tours. htm. Free, guided tours are offered throughout the day and last about forty-five minutes. Check with the Treasurer's Business Office on the first floor for times.

LOCATION 1100 N. Congress Ave.

PARKING Two hours of free public parking are available at the Visitor Parking Garage at 1201 San Jacinto St. (barring any special events). Curbside paid parking is also available along surrounding streets.

WEBSITE www.tspb.state.tx.us/SPB/Plan/Plan.htm

PHONE (512) 463-0063

HOURS Monday – Friday   7AM – 10PM
Saturday – Sunday   9AM – 8PM

ADMISSION Free

Thinkery: The New Austin Children's Museum

The only thing most children don't like about visiting this museum is leaving! As the museum touts, the space is perfect for children ages zero to eleven. The layout of the space offers plenty of room to explore, and exhibits attract kids by age and interest. As children develop, they explore new areas while discovering a variety of ways to interact with old favorites. All exhibits encourage multi-level learning and cooperation, while kids have a blast!

With the recent move into its new location in the Mueller development, this updated science and technology center now houses even more permanent exhibits to engage kids. These include a kitchen science lab, a hands-on inventor's workshop for young makers and builders, a healthy living market and Move! Studio, a cozy book nook, a space for nature play in the outdoor courtyard, and an aquatics discovery area, in addition to rotating exhibits.

Babies and toddlers can always find a safe haven to explore, protected from the excited bigger kids racing by, in sections of the Let's Grow and Currents exhibits reserved exclusively for them. During designated Baby Bloomer hours, babies and tots also have the run of the museum, as only three-year olds and younger are admitted. Special storytimes, sing-a-longs, and activities geared for young children are held.

The Thinkery also organizes regular storytimes (some bilingual), engineering projects, spring break and summer camps, and special events throughout the year. Check the online calendar for details.

LOCATION   1830 Simond Ave.

WEBSITE   www.thinkeryaustin.org

PHONE   (512) 469-6200

HOURS Tuesday – Friday   10AM – 5PM
Saturday – Sunday   10AM – 6PM
Monday closed (except for Baby Bloomers)

Baby Bloomer Hours *(for children 3 and under)*
Monday   9AM – noon
Saturday   9AM – 10AM

ADMISSION Free children 0-24 months
$9   visitors
$8   seniors
$7   military

Community Nights, Wednesday 5 – 8PM,
entrance by donation and free on Sunday
5 – 6PM

Torchy's Tacos

Torchy's redefines the taco. And the original business opened in a food trailer. It doesn't get much more Austin than that. While they can serve a basic breakfast taco that even the choosiest child will eat, they are even better at adding some heat and make some pretty mean combinations. Try smoked beef brisket with your potato and eggs,  or shrimp with cabbage slaw, cilantro, queso fresco, and jalapeño. Other tasty tacos include fried avocados, jalapeño sausage, blackened salmon, or fried portobello mushrooms wrapped with combinations of refried black beans, corn relish, poblano sauce, queso, or pico de gallo. Due to popular demand, this local taco joint has expanded to several locations, but their spot along Bouldin Creek in the South Austin Trailer Park and Eatery remains the most authentic—and the best for kids. Picnic tables cluster beneath shady trees, or you can eat in the rustic open-air wood and tin building with a t.v., foosball, and ping-pong. (It's one of the few trailer park eateries with restrooms too.) Other food trucks share the lot, so you might luck into some dessert or smoothies. But Torchy's is the flagship.

LOCATION 1311 S. 1st St.

WEBSITE www.torchystacos.com

PHONE (512) 366-0537

HOURS
Monday – Thursday	7AM – 10PM
Friday	7AM – 11PM
Saturday	8AM – 11PM
Sunday	8AM – 10PM

Tower Garden

When on the University of Texas campus with kids, the Tower Garden is worth seeking out. This series of ponds filled with fish, turtles, and lily pads will delight young children as they watch turtles pop up their heads to greet them or stack themselves on rocks to sun. The garden, which lies just north of the UT Tower, is dedicated to the memory of victims of the Tower Shooting of 1966, but most young visitors know it affectionately as the "Turtle Pond."

LOCATION Between 24th St. and the north side of the UT Tower (directly behind the Biological Laboratories building)

PARKING Two of the nearest visitor parking garages are the San Antonio Garage located three blocks west (25th St. and San Antonio St.) and the San Jacinto Garage (24th St. and San Jacinto Blvd.).

Toy Joy

Toy Joy is one of those rare places where all ages play together, testing out hula hoops and wacky costumes, goggling over 80s action heroes, or perusing the many bins of timeless party favors (made even more unique through clever and creative signage). Specializing in the fun and nostalgic, Toy Joy offers the latest in pop culture while staying true to old favorites: rubber animals, action figures, games and puzzles, puppets, pranks, and an entire wall dedicated to Hello Kitty and friends. Even grown-ups can test out inflatable Rody horses in a special corralled area. An added bonus is a trip to the Black Light Room filled with an amazing assortment of plastic animals, from the amphibious and reptilian to the terrestrial and aquatic. It's apparent that the owners and staff have fun with their inventory, and you'll find toys here that you won't find anywhere else in town.

LOCATION 403 W. 2nd St.

PARKING Curbside meter parking and several garages are available nearby. Toy Joy offers parking validation at some garages with a purchase. Call ahead to ask for the locations.

WEBSITE www.toyjoy.com

PHONE (512) 320-0090

HOURS Daily, 10AM – 9PM

Triangle Farmers' Market

A great mid-week market held year-round on Wednesdays, the Triangle not only has yummy, locally grown food, it also boasts live music and a big open field for dancing and playing. Pack balls, frisbees, a picnic blanket, and if you have water-loving kids, a towel and change of clothes for the splash pad. Grab a bite to eat from local vendors and hang out awhile. It's a perfect place for families to gather at the end of the day.

"Meet me at the SFC Farmers' Market
at Sunset Valley, Downtown
and The Triangle"

LOCATION 4600 N. Lamar Blvd.
The park is situated in the center of the Triangle's mixed-use development and is accessible from either 46th St. and Guadalupe St. or 46th St. and Lamar Blvd.

PARKING Free parking is available in the retail parking garage or along the streets.

WEBSITE www.sfcfarmersmarketthetriangle.org

HOURS Wednesday, 3PM – 7PM

Turkey Creek Trail

Primarily a wooded trail through the Texas Hill Country, kids will enjoy the level terrain, the shade provided by the canopy of trees, and the excitement of leaping on stepping stones across Turkey Creek, which the trail crosses at several spots. For parents, this trail offers the feel of getting out of the city without having to travel far. If you have a dog, bring the family pet along too. As a no-leash zone, this is a popular hike for dog owners.

The entire trail is 2.7 miles long. After ¾ of a mile, the trail splits and becomes a loop that moves from limestone creek bed surrounded by fern-covered canyon walls to a short climb to the top of a cliff for a brief walk through more arid, exposed Hill Country before heading back down into the trees to the original trail. With the exception of this one short climb, the hike is fairly level. The full length of the trail may be a bit much for little legs, but simply turn around at any point for a shorter outing. Or take a left where the trail splits to go to the Fern Wall and listen for the burble of flowing water or rest on a bench or boulder and just enjoy being out. The scenery makes any length trek worth the trip.

For restrooms, a picnic, or a swim in Lake Austin afterwards, drive 1 mile farther up City Park Road to *Emma Long Metropolitan Park*.

LOCATION 1600 City Park Rd.

PARKING Park in the dirt lot at the trailhead. Spots are most difficult to come by on weekend mornings when the trail is busiest.

WEBSITE www.austinparks.org/apfweb/park.php?parkId=666

TRAIL MAP www.austintexas.gov//sites/default/files/files/ Parks/GIS/EmmaLongKioskMap_TurkeyCk.pdf

ADMISSION Free

The Union Underground

You rarely see a bowling alley like this one—it glows. Walk down the steps of the Texas Union student center on the University of Texas campus and enter a bowling alley where disco balls and black lights illuminate toothy grins, neon-colored laces on bowling shoes, and neon pink, orange, and yellow bowling balls as they roll down the lanes. This alley features twelve lanes with programmable bumpers for younger bowlers, in addition to billiards, foosball, and air hockey. Families and college students tend to be the most common patrons, although the two groups' schedules rarely overlap so the lanes usually aren't crowded until after children's bedtimes. Snacks are available at the front desk (candy, ice cream bars, chips, and sodas), or head to the food court on the Union's main floor. While there's plenty of good bowling in Austin, this one adds a neat spin to the sport.

LOCATION Texas Union building at 24th St. and Guadalupe St. on the University of Texas campus, in the north corner of the bottom floor

PARKING San Antonio Garage (25th St. and San Antonio St.) is the nearest parking garage, one block away. The university is also well served by Capital Metro and has plenty of bike racks, so consider taking a bus, shuttle, or bikes to avoid the hassle of campus parking.

WEBSITE: www.utexas.edu/universityunions/texas-union/scene/underground

PHONE (512) 475-6670

HOURS Monday–Saturday 10AM–3AM
Sunday noon–3AM

Special Glow Ball Hours:

Thursday – Friday 5PM – 3AM
Saturday   10AM – 3AM
Sunday   noon – 3AM

The Union Underground observes the university schedule to some extent so call ahead around holidays and semester breaks to confirm times.

RATES **Regular bowling** (per game/per person)

$2.50 (Monday – Friday 10AM – 5PM)
$3.00 (Monday – Wednesday 5PM – close)

Glow Ball bowling (per game/per person)

$3.50 (Thursday – Friday 5PM – close
         and all day Saturday – Sunday)

Bowling shoe rentals

$1.50/pair (Monday – Friday 10AM – 5PM)
$2.00/pair (after 5PM & on weekends)

University of Texas Tower Tour

If you have ever been curious about the view from the UT Tower, tours take visitors up twenty-seven floors by elevator and three more by stairs to an observation deck that offers an amazing panorama of the city. Kids will like the bird's eye view of the University of Texas campus, the Capitol, downtown, and tree-filled neighborhoods and hills that stretch to the edge of town. Chest-high walls along the deck and metal railings that extend overhead make the area safe, although shorter children may need a boost to see out. Binoculars are for the borrowing and cameras and cell phones are permitted. Mid-way through the forty-five minute tour, guides offer a short talk to those interested about the architectural design and function of the building and then give groups a little more time to look around and ask questions before the tour's end.

Reservations are recommended. Visitors are advised to arrive twenty minutes early to pick up tickets from the Hospitality Center in the Texas Union. Tickets are released to those on the waitlist ten minutes prior to the tour. No purses, backpacks, or bags are allowed. Leave them behind, or you can rent a locker at the Hospitality Center for $1 to store your belongings.

LOCATION   Tours are in the Main Building on the University of Texas campus. Pick up tickets in the Texas Union (located on campus on Guadalupe St. between 22nd and 24th Sts.) at the Hospitality Center (on the south end of the main floor).

PARKING   Parking in the University Co-op garage at 23rd St. and San Antonio St.

WEBSITE   www.utexas.edu/tower

PHONE   (512) 475-6633

HOURS   The schedule varies with the university's calendar. Check the online schedule or call for tour days and times.

ADMISSION $6 per person

Veloway

Biking on smooth pavement in the Hill Country sans cars makes an outing to the Veloway worth the trip, especially for young bikers. The 3-mile loop (that can be shortened to 1 mile with a shortcut) winds through wooded scenic green space in the Circle C Metropolitan Park just up the street from the Lady Bird Johnson Wildflower Center. Open exclusively to cyclists and skaters, the trail runs one-way in a clockwise direction, with slower traffic staying to the right. Picnic tables and open areas along the way provide good rest stops, or keep pedaling and enjoy the fun of being on a road with only human-powered traffic. Portable toilets and a water fountain are located near the entrance.

LOCATION	4900 La Crosse Ave.
PARKING	Dirt parking lot on site.
WEBSITE	www.austinparks.org/apfweb/park.php?parkId=365
TRAIL MAP	www.ci.austin.tx.us/publicworks/downloads/veloway_map.pdf
HOURS	Daily, dawn to dusk
ADMISSION	Free

Walter E. Long Metropolitan Park at Decker Lake

Stretching along the southern end of Lake Walter E. Long, a sizeable 1,200-acre lake in east Austin (also called Decker Lake), this long slip of a park on the waterfront offers picnicking, swimming, and fishing with access points at several coves and inlets along the bank. If you come to fish, there is a bait shop just outside the park gate. Be sure to pick up a map and brochure from the entrance station that lists the most common types of fish caught as well as the state bag and length limits. A boat ramp and two docks are also located in the park, as well as several good spots for putting in a kayak or canoe.

LOCATION	6614 Blue Bluff Rd.
WEBSITE	www.austinparks.org/apfweb/park.php?parkId=370
PHONE	(512) 926-5230
HOURS	Daily, 7AM–10PM
ADMISSION	$5 per vehicle Monday–Thursday
	$10 per vehicle Friday–Sunday
	$1 per person walk-ins

Westcave Outdoor Discovery Center

One of the most beautiful trails in the area, this 1-mile hike provides enough ecological and terrain diversity to keep children's interests, from wandering along flat, flower-lined paths to a scenic overlook at the top of the Canyon Trail, down stone steps (hold onto the handrail) to the natural springs burbling into the Pedernales River. The highlight of the hike is a gorgeous, lush grotto and waterfall adjacent to the cavern that gives Westcave its name.

Two distinct ecosystems overlap along this hike, making it unique in that a wide variety of vegetation covers the trail, from cactus and wildflowers to lush ferns and brilliant mosses. The trees also range from ashe juniper and sycamore to impressive six hundred-year old bald cypresses classified in the giant sequoia and redwood families.

To protect the area, the trail is only accessible to the general public during guided tours on the weekends. The guide adds much to the trek, leading groups behind the waterfall and into the cave while helping spot the endangered golden-cheeked warbler who lives here in the spring. (Binoculars are available for loan from the Educational Learning Center.) The entire tour lasts approximately one hour and fifteen minutes. With the forty-five minute drive from Austin, the venture can turn into a half-day event, and one well worth it.

Some tips: Be sure to get there a little early as tours are limited to the first thirty people (although it's rare that a tour will be full). While you wait, have a picnic and scope out the Educational

Learning Center. Be sure to wear appropriate shoes for the hike too; the area near the waterfall can be a bit slippery. No pets are allowed in the park.

LOCATION 24814 Hamilton Pool Rd., Round Mountain

DIRECTIONS From Austin, take Hwy. 71 west to Bee Cave. Turn left onto Ranch Rd. 3238 (Hamilton Pool Rd.) at the traffic light. After 14 miles, you'll cross the Pedernales River. The entrance to the Preserve is the next gate to the right.

WEBSITE www.westcave.org/visit

PHONE (830) 825-3442

HOURS Tours are scheduled on Saturdays and Sundays at 10AM, noon, 2PM, and 4PM

ADMISSION Free children under 4
$5 children 4-12
$10 teens and adults
$25 family

Westcave Outdoor Discovery Center Star Party

Forty-five minutes west of downtown, Westcave Preserve gets fairly dark skies and hosts star parties several months of the year. Astronomers set up telescopes near the Environmental Learning Center shortly before dark. As the first stars of the night appear, they point out constellations and direct their telescopes to the moon, planets, star nebulas, and the Milky Way to give visitors a closer glimpse of the universe. Registration is required and limited to thirty guests so that everyone has an opportunity to use the telescopes. Bring chairs, snacks, drinks, and a flashlight.

LOCATION 24814 Hamilton Pool Rd., Round Mountain

DIRECTIONS From Austin, take Hwy. 71 west to Bee Cave. Turn left onto Ranch Rd. 3238 (Hamilton Pool Rd.) at the traffic light. After 14 miles, you'll cross the Pedernales River. The entrance to the Preserve is the next gate to the right.

WEBSITE www.westcave.org/events

PHONE (830) 825-3442

EMAIL info@westcave.org

HOURS Program begins at dark and lasts 2 hours. Time varies by month so check website or call for exact time.

ADMISSION $5   children (ages 4–12)
$10 adults
$25 families

Whole Earth Provisions

North and South Lamar locations

For a camping and adventure specialty store, Whole Earth offers a surprisingly amazing selection of quality toys—especially ones that teach about the outdoors or that get kids out in it. In fact, their toy section has been slowly expanding over the years, claiming more and more retail space. While this is the place to go for nature and science-related toys like kites, magnets, astronomy kits, bug collecting boxes, binoculars, butterfly nets, and volcanoes, you can also find puppets, baby-friendly items, art supplies, bath toys, and activity books. Whole Earth has a unique, well-culled book section too with fun, slightly offbeat picture books and plenty of science-related titles for all ages. It's a perfect store to buy gifts, stock up on travel kits for road trips, or go play around a bit. Another plus is the friendly staff who wholeheartedly embrace the company philosophy to "Have fun!"

LOCATION	**North**
	1014 N. Lamar Blvd.
PHONE	(512) 476-1414
HOURS	Monday–Friday 10AM–8PM
	Saturday 10AM–8PM
	Sunday 11AM–6PM
LOCATION	**South**
	Westgate Shopping Center
	4477 S. Lamar Blvd.
PHONE	(512) 899-0992
HOURS	Monday–Friday 10AM–9PM
	Saturday 10AM–9PM
	Sunday 11AM–6PM

The third location on San Antonio Street near the University of Texas is also a great store, but because it caters to college students, its toy selection is much smaller.

WEBSITE www.wholeearthprovision.com

Whole Foods Rooftop

There is a little-known playground atop the roof of the downtown Whole Foods Market. Pack up snacks or a meal from the store and take the stairs or elevator up a level. Shaded tables sit adjacent to a small wooden playground (best for young children) where families can dine, play, and enjoy the rooftop view.

LOCATION 525 N. Lamar Blvd.
(corner of 6th St. and Lamar Blvd.)

WEBSITE www.wholefoods.com/stores/lamar

PHONE (512) 542-2200

HOURS Daily, 7AM–10PM

Wild Basin Stargazing and Moonlighting Tours

All ages come out for these tours led by the Austin Astronomical Society, although the evenings are best suited for children with enough of an attention span to listen to a short informative talk full of interesting information about the solar system and what visitors are likely to see on the particular night. After this introduction, stargazers are led on a sunset hike to a scenic overlook to wait for dark. Wear close-toed shoes and bring a small flashlight if you have one (loaner flashlights are also available). Volunteers use laser pointers to highlight constellations as they appear and telescopes are set up around the grounds for getting a closer look at the moon, stars, and planets. Wild Basin astronomy programs are held several times a year. Reservations are recommended. Check the forecast as they are subject to cancellation on overcast nights.

Wild Basin Preserve also contains 2½ miles of hiking trails open daily to the public. So allow extra time before sunset if you'd like to fit in a hike too. The ¼- to ½-mile hike (depending on whether you choose the South or North access point) that leads to the Waterfall is the highlight of this series of trails. Pick up a map at the trailhead or in the Environmental Education Center.

LOCATION 805 N. Capital of Texas Hwy. *(Turn at the brown highway sign for the Wild Basin Preserve)*

WEBSITE http://think.stedwards.edu/wildbasin

PHONE (512) 327-7622

HOURS Typically begins an hour before sunset and lasts two to three hours. (Call ahead for specific dates and times, or check the "events" section of the website.)

Admission Free children under 5
          $3   children ages 5-12
          $5   teens and adults
          $3   seniors

ZACH Theatre

Recently remodeled, the Zachary Scott Theatre located along the banks of Lady Bird Lake is home to locally produced plays and musicals as well as those of international renown. Family-friendly shows are often performed in the intimate, 130-seat theater in the round, making the experience especially engaging for audiences. ZACH's emphasis on youth engagement with theater is apparent from their season schedule and educational outreach, in addition to the many classes and camps they offer throughout the year.

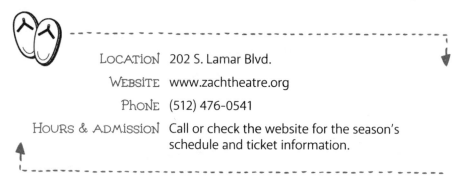

LOCATION   202 S. Lamar Blvd.

WEBSITE   www.zachtheatre.org

PHONE   (512) 476-0541

HOURS & ADMISSION   Call or check the website for the season's schedule and ticket information.

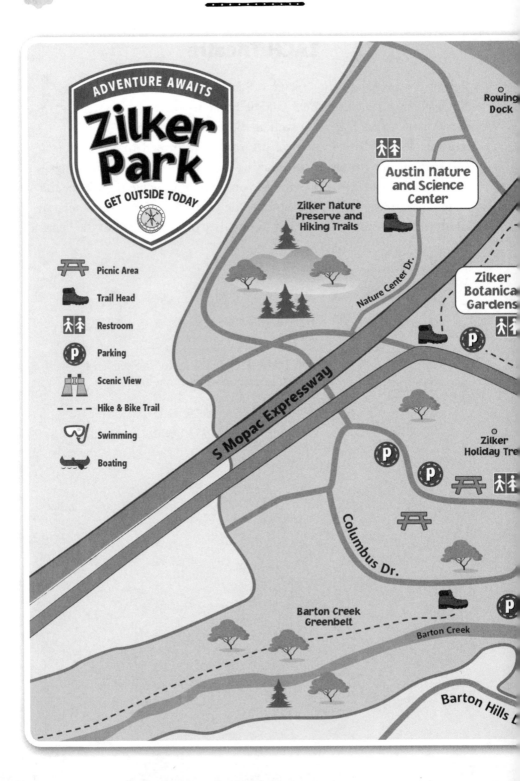

ADVENTURE AWAITS

Zilker Park

GET OUTSIDE TODAY

Picnic Area

Trail Head

Restroom

Parking

Scenic View

Hike & Bike Trail

Swimming

Boating

Rowing Dock

Austin Nature and Science Center

Zilker Nature Preserve and Hiking Trails

Nature Center Dr.

Zilker Botanica Gardens

S Mopac Expressway

Zilker Holiday Tre

Columbus Dr.

Barton Creek Greenbelt

Barton Creek

Barton Hills

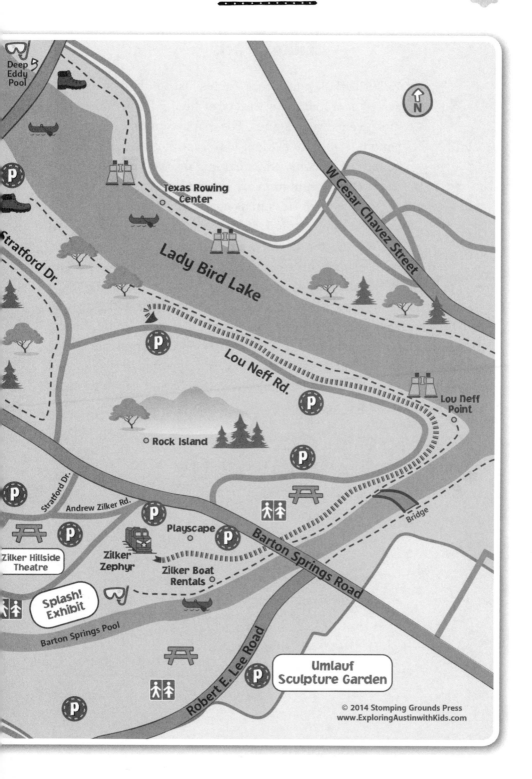

Deep Eddy Pool

Texas Rowing Center

W Cesar Chavez Street

N

Stratford Dr.

Lady Bird Lake

P

Lou Neff Rd.

P

Lou Neff Point

Rock Island

P

Stratford Dr.

P

Andrew Zilker Rd.

P

Playscape

P

Bridge

Zilker Hillside Theatre

Zilker Zephyr

Zilker Boat Rentals

Barton Springs Road

Splash! Exhibit

Barton Springs Pool

Robert E. Lee Road

Umlauf Sculpture Garden

P

Zilker Park

Zilker Park, located on 350 acres just south of downtown, serves as a hub for a variety of family-friendly activities and events year-round. The park contains a botanical garden, sculpture garden, playscape, soccer fields, nature center, educational water exhibit, disc golf course, hillside theater, miniature train, canoe and kayak rentals, and one of Austin's most treasured spots, Barton Springs Pool. The park backs up to the Hike and Bike Trail to the northeast and the Barton Creek Greenbelt to the south, making it feel even larger. (Detailed entries can be found for each of the activities mentioned above, and a *map* of the park is provided on pages 176–177.)

If you are simply looking for a good place to wander with the kids, head to the playscape area. From here, you can ride the train, have a picnic, watch swimmers plunge into Barton Springs from the diving board, or visit the Splash! Exhibit. Take the opportunity to descend the stairs nearby to play in the chilly water of Barton Creek where it overflows from Barton Springs Pool.

LOCATION   2100 Barton Springs Rd.

PARKING   Several parking lots are available (see map link from the webpage).

WEBSITE   www.austintexas.gov/department/zilker-metropolitan-park

HOURS   Daily, 5AM–10PM

ADMISSION   Free. Note that a $5 parking fee is charged on weekends and holidays from March through Labor Day for the parking lots off of Barton Springs Rd.

Austin Nature and Science Center

There is enough at this center to engage children for hours. So make a day of it, or break up the experience into several shorter outings. Restrooms, maps, and information are available in the Nature and Science Center's main building. Picnic tables for snacks or lunch can be found near the Trailhouse.

Austin Nature and Science Center

This building houses the Information Desk, the Naturalist Workshop, and Public Exhibits. Budding naturalists will enjoy the Workshop where the motto is "Come in—Please touch!" Magnifying glasses and a microscope are on hand for children to explore the plethora of bones, rocks, insects, shells, snake skins, and animal pelts that fill the tables and shelves. If your explorers have something interesting from nature, they can bring it to the Trade Counter and exchange their knowledge of it for points towards another item to take home with them (see Trade Counter hours below).

The public exhibits are just around the corner. Always interactive and science-related, the themes of these rotating exhibits range from the celestial to the terrestrial. The cave exhibit is a constant though. Kids can wander through to peek at bugs in the cave walls or try to identify the animals poised above. Behind the giant glass windows in this space kids also get an up-close view of the pond just outside.

Animal Exhibits

Exit the building to the back to find a stream-lined path that leads to the Animal Exhibits. Children can visit the resident coyote, bobcat, skunk, and raccoon, among other rescue animals. The Small Wonders building next door is home to smaller species. (Look up as you enter the building to find your first one!) Snakes, salamanders, toads, tarantulas, lizards, and birds make their homes here as well. Cross Nature's Way Drive to the Bird Sanctuary where hawks, buzzards, quail, and owls of all types roost.

Zilker Park Nature Preserve and Hiking Trails

Hikers can access the Preserve Hiking Trails through the Bird Sanctuary, or at two separate trailheads along Nature's Way Drive. See *Zilker Nature Preserve and Hiking Trails* for more details.

Dino Pit

This sand pile, the largest one in the city, hides dinosaur bones and skeletons waiting to be unearthed by young archaeologists. Shovels and brushes are provided, and educational signs about dinosaurs and the field of archaeology teach children more about their discoveries.

Classes and Camps

Check with the Information Desk for brochures on the latest happenings. Upcoming events and the *Natural Selections* and *Summer Camp* guides can also be found online. The Austin Nature and Science Center offers a variety of fun and educational classes for all ages, as well as family-friendly events year-round.

LOCATION	301 Nature Center Dr.
PARKING	Take Stratford Dr. in Zilker Park to a dirt parking lot under the Mopac Expy./Loop 1 bridge. Cross the street and head up the hill to the Nature and Science Center.
WEBSITE	www.austintexas.gov/department/austin-nature-and-science-center
PHONE	(512) 974-3888
HOURS	Monday – Saturday 9AM – 5PM
Sunday   noon – 5PM
Trade Counter hours:
Wednesday – Friday 10AM – 1PM
Saturday   10AM – 4PM
ADMISSION	Free

Barton Springs Pool

At 68 degrees, this natural, spring-fed pool along Barton Creek is *chilly*—and a mecca for Austinites of all ages who come to sunbathe on the grassy hillside, practice flips from the diving board, swim laps, or simply soak in the cool. It's a large pool with a section for floats on the lower end where water spills back into Barton Creek and a shallower section on the upper end below historic bathhouses. There is also plenty of room for lap swimming and snorkeling throughout. The shallow end is the best spot for kids where flat limestone slabs provide a sort of beach at the water's edge and the water is not quite as cold. Bring buckets, shovels, and water toys to play with.

LOCATION 2201 Barton Springs Dr.

PARKING Several parking lots are available in the park. A $5 parking fee is charged on weekends and holidays from March through Labor Day.

WEBSITE www.austintexas.gov/department/barton-springs-pool

PHONE (512) 867-3080

HOURS The pool is open year-round.

Fall-Spring hours:
Call or check the online schedule:
www.austintexas.gov/page/pools-splash-pads

Summer hours:
Friday – Wednesday 5AM – 10PM
Thursday   closed for cleaning

ADMISSION $1 children 11 and under
$2 juniors 12-17
$3 adults
$1 seniors
Non-resident admission is an additional $1.

Lou Neff Point

Young children flock to this spot along the Hike and Bike Trail at Lady Bird Lake to feed ducks, swans, geese, turtles, and fish. So bring your breadcrumbs! The pavilion at Lou Neff Point also provides a great vantage point for watching canoes and kayaks row by, with downtown as a backdrop.

LOCATION   2000 Lou Neff Rd.

PARKING   From Barton Springs Rd., turn onto Lou Neff Rd. and park in the first lot on the right. Head down to the Hike and Bike Trail along the lake and go left. It's a short walk to the pavilion.

ADMISSION   Free, with the exception of a $5 parking fee at Zilker Park on weekends mid-March through Labor Day weekend

Rowing Dock

The Rowing Dock is easy to spot from the Mopac bridge with its brightly-colored kayaks and stacks of rowing boats on Lady Bird Lake. This boathouse puts paddlers in on the quieter, less-trafficked west end of the lake. Head upriver beneath scenic cliffs and keep your eyes open for herons along the banks and stacks of turtles sunning themselves on logs. Kayaks, paddleboats, and stand-up paddleboards are available to rent by the hour. Onsite parking makes the dock easy to get to with kids, and a picnic table and portable restroom are on site. On nice weekends, boating can be a popular activity, so it's best to go early to avoid long waits. Bring a driver's license. Cubbies are available for storage.

LOCATION 2418 Stratford Dr. (just west of the Mopac Expy./Loop 1 bridge on Stratford Dr. Look for the blue and green painted poles and sign.)

PARKING Spaces are available in the gravel parking lot directly above the rental dock.

WEBSITE www.rowingdock.com

PHONE (512) 459-0999

HOURS **Summer hours**
Monday – Friday   8AM – 8PM (last rentals at 7PM)
Saturday – Sunday 7AM – 8PM (last rentals at 7PM)

Winter hours
Daily, 9AM – 6PM (last rentals at 5PM)

RATE Rentals range from $10 – $30/hour, or purchase a 6- or 10-punch card for lower rates. Cash or check only.

Splash! Exhibit

This exhibit is perfect for science-minded children of all ages. Interactive displays inside this simulated limestone cave allow them to test water quality, peer in fish and salamander tanks to see what swims in local creeks and rivers, pretend to navigate a mini-submarine in search of water contaminants, watch a short film about Barton Springs on a cave wall, and create thunderstorms at the push of a button to learn about human impact on watersheds. Even leaving is made fun as visitors exit through a sliding wall of bubbling water.

LOCATION	2201 Barton Springs Dr. (in the Sheffield Education Center to the right of the Barton Springs Pool entrance)
WEBSITE	www.austintexas.gov/department/beverly-s-sheffield-education-center
PHONE	(512) 481-1466
HOURS	Tuesday – Saturday 10AM – 5PM Sunday noon – 5PM Monday closed
ADMISSION	Free, with the exception of a $5 parking fee at Zilker Park on weekends mid-March through Labor Day weekend

Texas Rowing Center

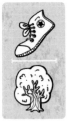

Situated along the Hike and Bike Trail at Lady Bird Lake, the Texas Rowing Center offers boat rentals, lessons, school programs, summer camps, and monthly events from fitness classes to full moon paddles. Friendly and helpful staff are ready to instruct or offer tips to get you on the water, whether your crew is heading out in a kayak, canoe, stand-up paddleboard, or rowing boat. Boaters can choose to go west and paddle beneath the Mopac bridge away from the crowds or set out towards the center of the lake, accompanied by ducks, swans, and turtles, for a view of downtown. Items you want to keep dry can be stored at the boathouse, along with keys or a driver's license. Portable restrooms are also onsite.

LOCATION 1541 W. Cesar Chavez St.
(The website offers detailed directions from a variety of access points)

PARKING Street parking is available along Stephen F. Austin Dr. Or park nearby in the gravel lot under the Mopac Expy./Loop 1 bridge, directly across the street from the Hike and Bike Trail.

WEBSITE www.texasrowingcenter.com

PHONE (512) 467-7799

HOURS Daily, 6AM – dusk

RATE Rentals range from $10–$25/hour or $25–$50/unlimited. Punch cards and unlimited use memberships are also a great deal for regular paddlers.

Umlauf Sculpture Garden

Featuring the works of Charles Umlauf, this beautiful outdoor museum combines art and nature seamlessly. Babies will enjoy the stroller ride beneath tall, shady cottonwoods and toddlers will be thrilled to roam along the gravel paths. Children of all ages will find the waterfall, streams, and ponds appealing as they cross bridges and wander pathways leading past strategically placed sculptures, from a cluster of intriguing animals to the boy "Diver" poised to plunge into the pond where a couple embraces in "The Kiss." Ask at the front desk for the scavenger hunt that transforms the exhibit into an engaging quest. Storytimes, family activities, tours, and art workshops for a range of ages are also offered throughout the year. Check the website or call for programs and dates.

LOCATION 605 Robert E. Lee Rd.

WEBSITE www.umlaufsculpture.org

PHONE (512) 445-5582

HOURS Wednesday – Friday 10AM – 4PM
Saturday – Sunday   noon – 4PM
Monday – Tuesday   closed

ADMISSION Free   children 12 and under
$5.00 teens and adults
$3.00 seniors (60+)

Zilker Botanical Gardens

The Botanical Gardens are a wonderful place to visit with children of all ages. With winding paths through flowers, ponds, butterflies, and even dinosaurs, visitors may roam for as long as they would like, or break up the experience into several short outings. Four areas with the most kid-appeal are listed below. Trail terrain varies with each section,  moving from pavement, to brick and stone, to decomposed granite, but the paths are stroller-friendly just about everywhere except the Japanese Garden. Maps and restrooms can be found at the Garden Center.

Japanese and Rose Gardens

The Japanese Garden lies just below and to the east of the Garden Center. Gentle streams flow alongside stone paths, through waterfalls, and into clear lily pad- and turtle-filled ponds. Parents will perceive the peacefulness of this garden while the secret pathways, stepping stones, wooden bridges, and bamboo overlooks on the trail make it exciting for children, full of pleasant discoveries.

Past the koi pond and gazebo, visitors enter the Rose Garden. From here, you can stay on the trail to follow metal dinosaur tracks on the

fence to the Prehistoric Garden, or head left to take the gently sloping sidewalk through terraced beds of roses and native flowers to the Pioneer Settlement and Butterfly Trail.

Pioneer Settlement and Butterfly Trail and Garden

A peek into the blacksmith shop, a furnished log cabin, and a one-room rural schoolhouse give children a glimpse into the lives of settlers from nearly two hundred years ago. On select weekends, blacksmiths fire up the furnace and offer living history demonstrations. Iron butterfly benches nearby provide a good resting spot and mark the beginning of a trail filled with flowers and springtime butterflies.

Hartman Prehistoric Garden

This garden is a favorite among children. As they follow the dinosaur tracks etched in the stones set along the circular pathways, their imaginations can run wild. Trekking through this simulated dinosaur "habitat" of palm trees, ferns, lily pads, and a waterfall, they will discover a large sculpture of a dinosaur feeding in the middle of a pond. If kids look closely, they may also discover non-extinct animals in the water too.

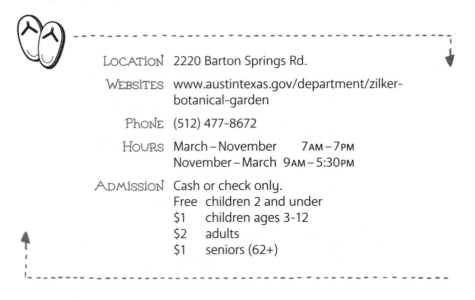

LOCATION 2220 Barton Springs Rd.

WEBSITES www.austintexas.gov/department/zilker-botanical-garden

PHONE (512) 477-8672

HOURS March – November   7AM – 7PM
November – March   9AM – 5:30PM

ADMISSION Cash or check only.
Free   children 2 and under
$1   children ages 3-12
$2   adults
$1   seniors (62+)

Zilker Nature Preserve and Hiking Trails

The Zilker Nature Preserve is one of those "smack dab in the middle of Austin" spots that has the power to make the city magically disappear as soon as you step into it. How far you can get along the trail with your little ones depends on their age, endurance, the temperature, and the length of their legs and attention spans. With the exception of the rock steps that lead down to the entrance of the main trailhead and a few switchbacks up to Lookout Point, the trails are mostly flat and easy. The entire area might be viewed as one large trail that takes hikers from one setting to another, from the shade of Texas mountain laurels and cottonwood trees to limestone cliffs topped with prickly pear cactus that overhangs creek beds to treks through sunny wildflower-filled meadows. But it is divided into a series of several short, marked trails with different access points. So you can always choose one for the day and take your time about it. Maps are posted at the trailheads.

Informational markers dot the area, along with reminders to children and their guides to:

Although absorbing the trail with all five senses might cause the rush of traffic from the nearby highway to rise in one's awareness, so will cricket chirps, song birds, hidden wildflowers, butterflies, the coolness of the shade, the heady scent of mulch from the trail, blooming cactus, and the excited voices of young children.

Trailheads

The **main trailhead** is located behind the *Austin Science and Nature Center* along Nature Center Drive. **Other access points** can be found (in geographical order heading south):

➤ Behind the Bird Sanctuary at the ANSC (open during the Center's hours)

➤ At the southwest end of Nature Center Drive

➤ Along Clubhouse Road (see "Parking" below)

Trails

Dry Creek: Stone steps lead hikers down into the trees to a dry, rocky creek bed. If you listen carefully, you'll hear the drip of water from the cliffs above.
Closest trailhead: Main trailhead

Hill Country Trail: An easy trail that crosses the Dry Creek a few times as it winds through native trees, grasses, and flowers.
Closest trailhead: Main trailhead

Mirror Pond: One of the best places for exploring, especially in the spring when the pond is filled with tadpoles, minnows, dragonflies, and frogs.
Closest trailhead: Bird Sanctuary

Meadows Trail: Trees give way to open fields of native grasses and flowers.
Closest trailhead: Bird Sanctuary

Lookout Point: Offers a gorgeous view of the Austin skyline beyond Zilker Park.

Closest trailhead: Clubhouse Road

Because the trails are part of a nature preserve, no dogs are allowed.

LOCATION Behind the Nature and Science Center at 301 Nature Center Dr.

PARKING Park in the lot under the Mopac Expy./Loop 1 bridge on Stratford Dr. Cross the street and head up the hill to the Austin Nature and Science Center. Two trailheads lie directly behind the Center along Nature Center Dr. Another can be found through the Bird Sanctuary.

Parking is also available at the picnic area along Rollingwood Dr. Directly across the street from the picnic tables, Clubhouse Rd. will lead you to the trailhead for Lookout Point that connects to the other trails below.

ADMISSION Free

Zilker Park Boat Rentals

This small wooden boathouse that sits along the trail just below Barton Springs Pool rents canoes, kayaks, and stand-up kayaks or paddleboards. The water is refreshingly chilly, with water circulating from nearby springs, and it's a fine spot for putting in. Head downstream with turtles, ducks, swans, and fellow boaters to cross under two bridges on your way from Barton Creek to Lady Bird Lake. Where the creek and lake meet, you'll find a great view of downtown.

While one hour rentals—with canoes fitting two adults and two small children—are typically long enough for most families, if you'd like to go longer or have a bigger group, check the website for "two for one" coupons. Bring a photo ID and cash. There are no lockers or storage areas. So travel light, or pack a waterproof bag to keep things dry, and as the attendants advise, "don't rock the boat."

LOCATION 2100 Barton Springs Rd.
below Barton Springs Pool

(Take the steps near the Zilker playscape
down to the creek. The trail at the bottom
leads to the boat rentals.)

PARKING Parking lots are available in Zilker Park. Note
that a $5 parking fee is charged in the park
on weekends from mid-March through Labor
Day weekend.

WEBSITE www.zilkerboats.com

PHONE (512) 478-3852

HOURS **Spring, Summer, Early Fall hours:**
Monday – Friday   10AM – dark
Saturday – Sunday   9AM – dark

Late Fall and Winter hours:
Nice weekends   11AM – dark

ADMISSION Cash only.
$12/hour
$40/day

Zilker Park Playscape

Featuring an old fire truck for playing in, a music area with xylophones, a sand pile, concrete sculptures for climbing on, swings, and a large playscape, this playground is a kid's paradise and one of the larger ones in Austin. The train tracks for the Zilker Zephyr divide the area in half. One of the most popular spots is on a bridge over the tracks, where children wave to passengers on the train as it runs beneath them. While the layout of the playground can create quite a challenging obstacle course for parents trying to keep up with everyone, it's a fun one for children of all ages.

LOCATION 2100 Barton Springs Rd.

PARKING Note a $5 parking fee is charged on weekends and holidays from March through Labor Day.

WEBSITE www.austintexas.gov/department/zilker-metropolitan-park

ADMISSION Free

Zilker Zephyr

There is something ageless about riding the Zilker Zephyr. Babies, toddlers, young children, parents, and grandparents enjoy the simple excitement and rhythm of it as life slows down to the pace of a miniature train. The Zephyr makes a twenty-five minute loop from the station through the north end of the park. Along the route, passengers can look for turtles, fish, ducks, and swans in Lady Bird Lake while passing under the bridge on Barton Springs Road. The track continues above the hike and bike trail with scenic views of the lake, park, and downtown. Most exciting for the kids is the home stretch where the train slips beneath a bridge on the Zilker playscape and through a tunnel before returning to the train depot.

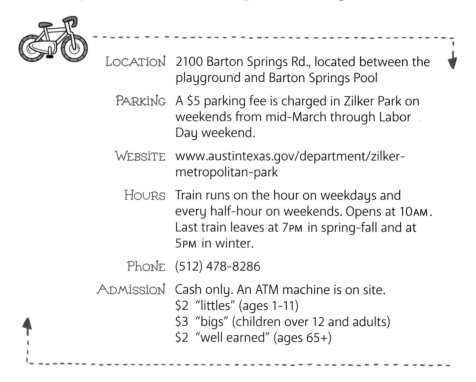

LOCATION 2100 Barton Springs Rd., located between the playground and Barton Springs Pool

PARKING A $5 parking fee is charged in Zilker Park on weekends from mid-March through Labor Day weekend.

WEBSITE www.austintexas.gov/department/zilker-metropolitan-park

HOURS Train runs on the hour on weekdays and every half-hour on weekends. Opens at 10AM. Last train leaves at 7PM in spring-fall and at 5PM in winter.

PHONE (512) 478-8286

ADMISSION Cash only. An ATM machine is on site.
$2 "littles" (ages 1-11)
$3 "bigs" (children over 12 and adults)
$2 "well earned" (ages 65+)

Annual Events

- Events Calendar
- Annual Festivals and Events

Events Calendar

January

Ice Skating at Whole Foods

February

Juggle Fest

March

Explore UT
Zilker Kite Festival
Rodeo Austin

April

Austin Family Music Festival at Pioneer Farms
Muster Days at Camp Mabry
Austin Dragon Boat Festival and Race
Eeyore's Birthday Party

May

Shakespeare in the Park

June

Children's Day Art Park
Nature Nights at the Lady Bird Johnson Wildflower Center

July

Children's Day Art Park
Beverly S. Sheffield Zilker Hillside Theatre Summer Musical

July *(continued)*

Music Under the Star Concert Series at Bob Bullock

Nature Nights at the Lady Bird Johnson Wildflower Center

August

Beverly S. Sheffield Zilker Hillside Theatre Summer Musical

Lake Travis Hot Air Balloon Flyover

September

Austin Museum Day

October

Texas Book Festival

Crowe's Nest Farm Fall Family Fun Fest

Día de Los Muertos Viva La Vida Fest

November

Chuy's Children Giving to Children Parade

Ice Skating at Whole Foods

December

Ice Skating at Whole Foods

Holiday Sing-Along and Downtown Stroll

Austin Trail of Lights

Zilker Holiday Tree

Christmas Lights on 37th Street

Luminations at Lady Bird Johnson Wildflower Center

Austin Dragon Boat Festival and Race

This cultural event will captivate the attention of children and their parents as teams of rowers fly by in boats decked out like dragons during the daylong races on Lady Bird Lake. Families can watch from beneath the trees along the banks or on the docks for a closer view. Another highlight are the all-day performances by children's groups and local organizations representing a range of Asian cultures, from Hawaiian dances and Japanese Taiko drums to martial arts and Chinese dragon dances. There are plenty of booths with free children's activities and prizes. Delicious traditional foods are available at vendor booths too, healthier and tastier than typical festival fare. The event is an interesting, wonderful way to spend the morning alongside the lake while exploring Asian culture.

DATE	Last Saturday in April
TIME	Varies (check website)
LOCATION	2101 Bergman St. at Festival Beach along Lady Bird Lake
PARKING	Parking lots are available along the stretch of the park as well as street parking nearby.
WEBSITE	www.asianamericancc.com
ADMISSION	Free

Austin Family Music Festival

While Austin City Limits Fest has a kids' stage and the South by Southwest Music Festival includes family-friendly shows, this festival is unique in that it's *for* children. Kid-friendly bands play at two stages all day on the grounds of Pioneer Farms. Young musicians-to-be can stop by the Instrument Petting Zoo to create their own sounds, hop on a Musical Hayride, or take a trip in a horse-drawn wagon down dirt paths that lead past fiddle players at the old homestead, wandering bagpipers, and donkeys, longhorns,

and chickens making their own brand of music.

Families can also wander the ninety acres of **Pioneer Farms'** living history park to explore the blacksmith shop, the animals in Symphony Barn, a Tonkawa Indian camp, and old homesteads where volunteers in period costume reenact life on a Texas farm in the mid-1800s. Children's activities and concessions are available too.

DATE	Saturday in April
TIME	Typically 10AM – dusk (check website)
LOCATION	Pioneer Farms at 10621 Pioneer Farms Dr.
WEBSITE	www.austinfamilymusicfestival.com
ADMISSION	$12/person in advance

Austin Museum Day

 Austin Museum Day features free admission to dozens of participating museums with special events planned all day. It poses the perfect opportunity to pop into all of those you have been wanting to visit and do a museum tour of Austin. Or head to your favorite one to see what exciting activities or new exhibits have been added for the day. Check the website for locations and a schedule of events.

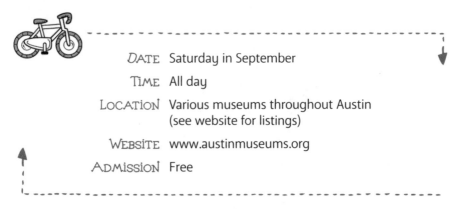

DATE   Saturday in September

TIME   All day

LOCATION   Various museums throughout Austin
(see website for listings)

WEBSITE   www.austinmuseums.org

ADMISSION   Free

Austin Trail of Lights

An Austin tradition, the Trail of Lights Festival attracts huge crowds during the holiday season. It stretches along the north end of Zilker Park with dozens of classic and contemporary holiday scenes lighting the way. Concessions are available and live music plays. While you're there, be sure to visit the ***Zilker Holiday Tree*** across the street. Turnout is heavy for this popular event, so go early and expect crowds.

DATE	Two weeks during the Christmas holidays
TIME	7PM–10PM
LOCATION	2100 Barton Springs Rd.
PARKING	Limited paid parking is available in the park. (Be sure to note road closures during the Trail of Lights.) Off-site shuttles are also available from several locations around town for a minimal fee.
WEBSITES	www.austintrailoflights.org
ADMISSION	Free

Beverly S. Sheffield Zilker Hillside Theatre

Theater patrons of all ages spread their blankets on the grassy hillside on warm summer nights to watch Broadway musicals and Shakespeare under the stars. It's a wonderful, magical way to introduce children to theater in a relaxed setting. Go early (anytime after 6PM) to secure a good spot, then let the kids roam the hill and explore. Or pack a picnic to enjoy at sunset as you watch the show. Snacks and drinks can also be purchased from the concession stand. The performances begin at dusk and run rather late, so bring a pillow and blanket for the young ones as they drift to sleep to some of the best bedtime stories ever.

DATE   Shakespeare in May; Musical from July – August

TIME   Dusk (approximately 8PM)

LOCATION   2206 William Barton Dr. in Zilker Park across from Barton Springs Pool

WEBSITE   http://austintexas.gov/department/zilker-hillside-theater

PHONE   (512) 477-5335

ADMISSION   Free, donations accepted. Note that a $5 parking fee is charged to park in Zilker Park on weekends during the summer months.

Children's Day Art Park

You can spot these weekly concerts from blocks away. Just follow the line of strollers, toddlers, and young children making their way towards the beautiful limestone amphitheater at Symphony Square where balloons, bubbles, and music fill the air. Children's musicians perform each week, along with clowns, mimes, and storytellers. Afterwards, concertgoers wind their way up Waller Creek to the historic Austin Symphony building and courtyard where face painters and storytellers set up shop on the lawn, lemonade is ten cents a cup, and an Art Tent is filled with free activities. Due to the popularity of this annual family-friendly event, it's best to get there early to find parking nearby. Stroller parking is available at the entrance.

DATES   Wednesday mornings in June and July

TIME   9:30AM   Gates open for Instrument Petting Zoo
and activities

10AM   Performances begin followed by Art
Tent Activities

11:30AM   Event ends

LOCATION   Symphony Square Amphitheater at
1101 Red River St.

PARKING   Curbside meter parking is available, or park
in the Capitol Visitor Parking garage located
between Trinity St. and San Jacinto Blvd. and
12th and 13th Sts.

WEBSITE   www.austinsymphony.org/events/childrens-
day-art-park

ADMISSION $.50   child
Free   adults accompanied by a child

Christmas Lights on 37th Street

If you're on the lookout for good Christmas lights, bundle up the kids and grab some hot chocolate. Then head to 37th Street, an eclectic mix of funky, historic bungalows, where you never know what you'll find, but you can be sure it will be uniquely festive and quintessentially Austin. Fairly near the University of Texas campus, neighbors on this block go all out, with lights stretching communally across the street from rooftop to rooftop, houses wrapped (literally) in brilliant glows, and yards filled with creative scenes from sock monkey nativities to political satires to giant metal dinosaurs and stuffed animal petting zoos… all covered in lights. You're likely to come across residents playing live Christmas music in their front yards or greeting the stream of thousands of holiday goers who pass by each season. Park the car and walk so you take in the scenes on both sides of the block and even wander to some of the backyards lit for the occasion.

DATE   Typically mid-December through Christmas

LOCATION   The block of 37th St. east of Guadalupe St. Traffic is one-way onto 37th St. and often backs up for the event. Consider parking on a nearby street and walking.

ADMISSION   Free

Chuy's Children Giving to Children Parade

Held on the Saturday of Thanksgiving weekend, the Chuy's parade marks a fun way to begin the Christmas holidays with the spirit of giving. Children donning reindeer antlers and jingle bells sit in strollers and perch atop parents' shoulders as their favorite characters float down the street on giant, inflatable balloons, interspersed with marching bands, classic cars, Santa's sleigh, and festive floats. At one point, the procession stops for onlookers bearing gifts to load truck beds and trailers with their goodies for other boys and girls. All donations go to Operation Blue Santa.

DATE   Saturday after Thanksgiving

TIME   Typically 11AM (lasts about one hour)

LOCATION   Congress Ave. (from the State Capitol to Cesar Chavez St. Check website for possible changes to the route.)

PARKING   City Hall parking garage (on Lavaca St. between 1st and 2nd Sts.) or curbside meter parking.

WEBSITE   www.chuysparade.com

ADMISSION   Free

Crowe's Nest Farm Fall Family Fun Fest

See Crowe's Nest Farm entry under the "Places to Go" section

DATE Saturday in October

LOCATION 10300 Taylor Ln., Manor

WEBSITE www.crowesnestfarm.org

PHONE (512) 272-4418

HOURS & ADMISSION Call for event times and admission prices.

Día de Los Muertos Viva La Vida Fest

Hosted by Mexic-Arte Museum, this annual cultural festival honors the memories of loved ones through a lively, grand celebration of life in the Latin American tradition. Fun, educational family activities and live entertainment begin in the afternoon at Plaza Saltillo where kids can learn more about the Day of the Dead traditions through interactive, hands-on projects. At dusk, a Grand Procession moves the event downtown through a vibrant parade of puppets, props, floats, and costumed participants. Crowds line the route along East Sixth Street to watch. At the end of the procession, the festival continues in all its vitality with a street celebration featuring live music and dance performances. Mexican and Tex-Mex food and drink vendors also set up tasty booths for the evening.

DATE	Typically one of the last two weekends in October or the first weekend in November
TIME	2PM–10PM
LOCATION	2PM–6PM Saltillo Plaza at E. 5th St. and Comal St. 6PM–7PM Grand Procession down E. 6th St. to Downtown 7PM–10PM Downtown on 5th St. from Congress Ave. to Brazos St.
WEBSITE	www.mexic-artemuseum.org
PHONE	(512) 480-9373
ADMISSION	Free

Eeyore's Birthday Party

Eeyore's is a unique phenomenon. Originating in the 1960s with University of Texas students celebrating the birthday of the A.A. Milne character Eeyore the donkey, the event has come to attract college students, hippies of all ages, families, and anyone with an appreciation for the fun and truly wacky. Live music plays, a drum circle beats all day, and outlandish costumes abound. If you forget yours, you can count on the face painting, temporary tattoo, and colored hair spray booths to get you festive.

It's best to get there early in the day when the Children's Area is open and the event is more family-friendly (before the crowd grows and some of the more eccentric costumes include little more than body paint). Free crafts and activities are available as well as ticketed game booths with prizes. Children can pet a live donkey, head to the playground, or participate in the egg toss, costume contest, and potato sack race. Food and drink vendors are also on the grounds, as is a general feeling of communal celebration.

DATE	Last Saturday in April (rain date is the following Saturday)
TIME	Children's Area typically runs 11AM–4PM; party ends at dark
LOCATION	Pease Park, 1100 Kingsbury St.
PARKING	Parking in the nearby neighborhoods fills up, so get there early or consider walking, biking or taking a shuttle. See website for shuttle locations.
WEBSITE	www.eeyores.com
ADMISSION	Free

Explore UT

Explore UT invites children of all ages to step foot onto a college campus for a day and imagine the possibilities. Over fifty thousand visitors come from across the state to participate in the four hundred programs and activities for kids—from rockets, robots and steamroller art to fashion, film, forensics, and face painting. Open-air booths, exhibits, and performances span the University of Texas' Forty Acres. Schedules are available online and at the event for those who would like to carefully plot out their day from the many classes and activities offered both inside and outside of the classrooms. Considering the campus-wide scope of the event, families can also simply wander and find plenty to see and do. It's an amazingly well-orchestrated production put on by the university to introduce Texas children to the world of college.

DATE   First Saturday of March

TIME   Typically 11AM–5PM (check website)

LOCATION   University of Texas at Austin

PARKING   Garages available on campus (see www.utexas.edu/parking/maps/visitor/ or check the event website for parking recommendations). Several Capital Metro bus routes also service UT.

WEBSITE   www.utexas.edu/events/exploreut

ADMISSION   Free

Holiday Sing-Along and Downtown Stroll

For a wonderful event to begin the holiday season, grab your homemade sleds and head over to the Capitol for the annual tree lighting ceremony. Who says you can't have winter fun in Texas without snow? Kids spill over the rolling landscape of the Capitol grounds on cardboard sleds as crowds gather at the footsteps of the building to sing Christmas carols. At the appointed hour, everyone awaits the lighting of the forty-foot Christmas tree at the south gate. Festivities then continue along Congress Avenue to the Second Street District where retailers, cultural centers, and museums open their doors for extended hours and special events. Check the website for the full schedule.

DATE	First Saturday in December
TIME	Typically 6PM – 9PM
LOCATION	1100 N. Congress Ave.
WEBSITE	www.downtownaustinholidays.com
PHONE	(512) 469-0476
ADMISSION	Free

Ice Skating at Whole Foods

For urban, outdoor ice skating in Texas during the holiday season, check out the temporary rink on the roof of the downtown Whole Foods Market. Dress warm. It gets chilly! Wristbands are sold at a specified checkout lane in the store and skate rentals are located upstairs. The rink is fairly small but offers fun rooftop skating with a view. Head downstairs to the café for hot chocolate afterwards.

DATES Holiday season (Saturday after Thanksgiving through mid-January)

TIME Call or check the website for this year's skate schedule (typically 9AM or 10AM until dark)

LOCATION 525 N. Lamar Blvd.

WEBSITE www.wholefoodsmarket.com/stores/lamar

PHONE (512) 542-2200

ADMISSION $10 person, including skate rentals

Juggle Fest

Sitting in an auditorium with a crowd of giggling children enthralled by juggling balls, rings and cones, circus acts, and pure zaniness is not a bad way to spend the evening. The Public Show put on by the Texas Juggling Society as part of its three-day Juggle Fest features performers from all over the country and is filled with silliness, fun, and magic. Hearkening back to an older time in entertainment, it's perfect theater for kids. For those with an aspiring juggler in the family, purchase a wristband for the entire weekend event of workshops, games, and insider tips.

DATE   Weekend in February

TIME   Workshops are held Friday evening and all day Saturday and Sunday. The Public Show happens Saturday night (typically 7:30PM. See website for schedule of events.)

LOCATION   1102 S. Congress Ave. at Texas School for the Deaf

WEBSITE   www.juggling.place.org/jugglefest

ADMISSION   *(subject to change)*
$10   Ticket for Public Show for ages 6 and up
$20   Wristband for entire festival (includes shows)
One-day passes and family gym packs are also available.

Lake Travis Hot Air Balloon Flyover

Early risers in the family will enjoy this annual gathering of Central Texas balloonists who lift off over Lake Travis in colorful hot air balloons as the sun hits the horizon. Arriving before sunrise, they unload in a large field adjacent to Mansfield Dam as spectators set up chairs to watch the event unfold. Others wander the grounds to get up-close views as teams lay their balloons out flat on the ground before filling them with air to towering heights. Pilots then

 step into the wicker baskets, release a few blasts of flame from the burners, and rise into the air. This process continues until all dozen or so balloons have launched. It can be difficult to track them once they are off (as the winds determine the flight path), and the event goes rather quickly but it's an impressive experience worth the trip.

DATE First Saturday in August

TIME Sunrise

LOCATION 4370 Mansfield Dam Rd.
Balloons launch from a space adjacent to Mansfield Dam, just past Mansfield Dam Park. Pass the park and continue straight where the road loops around a small grassy area. This is the launching site. Visitors are welcome on foot here, but park in the designated parking areas or along the road.

PARKING Parking is available in the lot on site or along the entrance road.

WEBSITE www.centraltexasballooning.org

PHONE (512) 481-2822

ADMISSION Free

Luminations at the Lady Bird Johnson Wildflower Center

The *Lady Bird Johnson Wildflower Center* softly glows with thousands of luminarias and twinkling lights for this annual holiday event. Bring glow sticks or small flashlights and climb the Observation Tower for a beautiful view of the grounds from above. Local performers play live music all evening. Kids can head to the Visitors Center and the Little House for Christmas nature crafts and children's activities. Hot chocolate and goodies are available in the Café. It's a beautiful way to begin the holiday season.

DATE   Early/mid-December weekend

TIME   6PM – 9PM

LOCATION   4801 La Crosse Ave.

WEBSITE   www.wildflower.org/luminations

PHONE   (512) 232-0100

ADMISSION   Free with canned food donations

Music Under the Star Concert Series

Bring lawn chairs or picnic blankets to set up on the plaza of the Bob Bullock Texas State History Museum for family-friendly Friday evenings in July filled with free live music by an impressive lineup of local artists. Past performances have ranged from Western swing and Big Band to Latino rock, Celtic music, Polka, Ragtime, Blues, and everything in-between. Free food, drinks, and desserts are for the picking until supplies run out. Paid concessions and a cash bar are also on hand. It's best to get there early before the lines get long. If the heat gets to you after dancing on a warm summer evening and you need more than iced tea to cool you down, head into the air-conditioned museum to explore the three floors of exhibits. Admission is on the house for these nights.

DATES	Friday evenings in July
TIME	6PM – 9PM
LOCATION	1800 N. Congress Ave. (at the intersection of Martin Luther King, Jr. Blvd.)
PARKING	During the event, free parking is available in the museum's parking garage at the corner of 18th St. and Congress Ave.
WEBSITE	www.TheStoryofTexas.com
PHONE	(512) 936-8746
ADMISSION	Free

Muster Days at Camp Mabry

During this annual event in honor of our military, visitors are invited to tour the extensive grounds of *Camp Mabry* in army vehicles, climb aboard aircrafts on display, watch an Air Show, and explore the Texas Military Forces Museum or the tanks on Artillery Row. Military men and women dressed in period uniform share history from the Civil War to present day from historically recreated military camps around the base. As part of the educational mission of the event, impressive living history demonstrations and reenactments are scheduled throughout the weekend. (Check online for the schedule of events.) Fun children's activities, food booths, and live music further add to this American Heroes Celebration. Though most will leave with further appreciation for our men and women in uniform, children fascinated by all things military will be especially impressed by this event.

DATE   Mid-April on Muster weekend

TIME   Call or check the online schedule

LOCATION 2210 W. 35th St.
          The public entrance to Camp Mabry is off of
          35th St., just west of Mopac Expy./Loop 1.
          Drive half a mile past the old main gate
          (now barricaded), through the light at
          Exposition Blvd. At the bottom of the hill, just
          before a flashing traffic signal, turn right onto
          Maintenance Dr. to the gated entrance.

WEBSITE   www.texasmilitaryforcesmuseum.org

PHONE   (512) 782-5659

ADMISSION Free

Nature Nights at Lady Bird Johnson Wildflower Center

Nature Nights are a series of educational events held during the summer months at the **Lady Bird Johnson Wildflower Center**. They are dedicated to teaching children about a particular aspect of Texas ecology, plants, or animals—from butterflies, bees, and frogs to birds of prey, snakes, and fossils. The Center is a beautiful place to spend the evening as kids learn through hands-on activities, crafts, expert-led hikes or hunts, musical guests, and activities related to the specific topic. A well-organized program that is lots of fun, kids have the run of the place on these nights, but their grown-ups might just learn something new too. Check the schedule for the weekly themes.

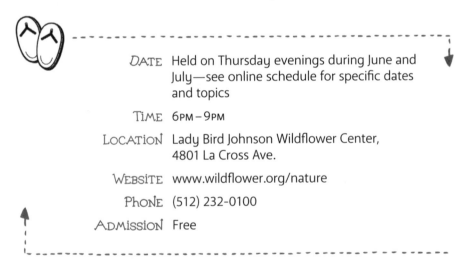

DATE   Held on Thursday evenings during June and July—see online schedule for specific dates and topics

TIME   6PM – 9PM

LOCATION   Lady Bird Johnson Wildflower Center, 4801 La Cross Ave.

WEBSITE   www.wildflower.org/nature

PHONE   (512) 232-0100

ADMISSION   Free

Rodeo Austin

The Star of Texas Fair and Rodeo is a tradition all ages will enjoy. Families can wander the Fairgrounds in a relaxed atmosphere while listening to country music (often live) and check out Ol' McDonald's Barn where cattle, pigs, sheep, turkeys, and rabbits wait to be shown and baby chicks totter about in the Hatchery. In nearby Kidstown, young cowboys and cowgirls can saddle up on ponies, visit the petting zoo, or watch milking demonstrations. Shows are often held around the grounds, from puppets to pig

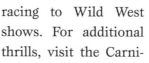

racing to Wild West shows. For additional thrills, visit the Carnival, a large expanse of rides where kids can roam for hours riding miniature trains, slides, roller coasters, and ferris wheels. The pro-rodeo events (including steer wrestling, barrel racing, bull riding, clowns, and more) begin each evening and conclude with a live concert in the Luedecke Arena. Food and drinks are available from a variety of vendors.

DATE Two weeks, mid-March

TIME Varies by day (check the online schedule). The Fairgrounds and Carnival open early. Rodeo events and concert begin in the evening.

LOCATION Travis County Expo Center at 9100 Decker Lake Rd.

WEBSITE www.rodeoaustin.com

PHONE (512) 919-3000

ADMISSION Check the website for online ticket discounts

Parking fee: $10

Fairgrounds only:
Free children under 2
$5   children ages 2-12
$8   teens and adults

Carnival:
$30   child unlimited ride wristband
$33   adult unlimited ride wristband

Advanced ticket prices. Tickets at the gate are $5 more. Or pay Fairgrounds admission and buy tokens for rides.

Rodeo & Concert tickets (includes Fairgrounds):
Tickets range from $20-$175 depending on seats

Shakespeare in the Park

Each year, the Austin Shakespeare theater troupe performs one of the bard's plays in *Zilker Park* for the month of May. The productions are wonderful and typically provide a modern twist on the works. It's a great way to expose children to Shakespeare, as audiences watch from the grassy hillside. While the Shakespearean language might pose a challenge for keeping the attention of the youngest ones, energetic children can always roam the hill (glow sticks add to the excitement of the night and make it easier to keep up with them) or sleepy kids can relax on a blanket and stargaze while listening to the poetry of the language. Arrive early to set up a blanket close to the stage. Bring a cooler with drinks and dinner too, or grab snacks at the concession stand. Portable restrooms are located nearby.

DATE	Thursdays through Sundays in May
TIME	Performances begin at 8PM
LOCATION	2206 William Barton Dr., Beverly S. Sheffield Zilker Hillside Theater in Zilker Park (across from Barton Springs Pool)
WEBSITE	www.austinshakespeare.org
PHONE	(512) 479-9491
ADMISSION	Free, donations accepted. Note that there is a $5 fee to park in the Zilker lots on weekends.

Texas Book Festival

Riding into town each October, authors, illustrators, publishers, booksellers, and bibliophiles of all ages take over the *Texas State Capitol*. They line up tents of books along its grounds and fill its chambers with readings, book signings, author panels, storytimes, food, children's entertainment, and live music. Recognizing an avid readership (or at the very least, devoted picture book fans) among younger types with unbridled curiosity and shorter attention spans, there are plenty of activities to keep kids engaged in the Children's Read Me a Story Tent, Children's Activity Tent, and Children's Entertainment Tent. The book selections for kids are as wide ranging as the acts, which in years past have included puppets, magic shows, drawing lessons, and science experiments. Young adult readers can browse the latest titles or attend talks by some of their favorite authors. (Check the schedule of events for activities and times.) The festival location also provides the perfect opportunity to tour the Capitol or have a picnic on the open lawn while taking in the scene in celebration of books.

DATE	Weekend in October
TIME	Typically 10AM – 5PM (although Lit Crawl for grown-ups runs much later)
LOCATION	Texas State Capitol (1100 Congress Ave.) and nearby venues (check schedule)
PARKING	Curbside meter parking is available on nearby streets (free on Sundays). Parking is also available in the Capitol Visitors Parking Garage with entrances on 12th and 13th Sts. between Trinity St. and San Jacinto Blvd.
WEBSITE	www.texasbookfestival.org
PHONE	(512) 477-4055
ADMISSION	Free

Zilker Holiday Tree

Since 1967, Austinites of all ages have been dizzily whirling in circles under this 155-foot "tree" of lights. Strings of colorful bulbs spiral down from one of Austin's original Moon Towers that illuminated the city back in the late 1800's. Topped by a 150-bulb star, it's quite an impressive sight. The Zilker Tree is traditionally lit from the first Sunday in December through the end of the year. (You might consider combining this outing with the *Austin Trail of Lights*.)

DATE   Check website for the date and time of the official Tree Lighting ceremony. The Zilker Tree stays lit at nights until December 31st.

TIME   6PM – midnight

LOCATION   2201 Barton Springs Dr.

PARKING   Free (except during the weeks of the Austin Trail of Lights when limited paid parking is available in the park as well as off-site shuttles from several locations around town for a minimal fee. Be sure to note road closures during this time.)

WEBSITE   www.austintexas.gov/department/zilker-holiday-tree

ADMISSION   Free

Zilker Kite Festival

This festival has celebrated the simple joy of springtime kite flying since 1929, making Austin home to the longest continuously running kite festival in the country. *Zilker Park* is dedicated to kite flyers and picnickers on this day. Contests for the highest flying, smallest, steadiest, biggest, and most unusual kites are held in the competitors' field. Vendors offer food, drinks, and children's activities nearby.

If you're willing to wait in line, a ride on the *Zilker Zephyr* offers a neat view of the entire event. With attendance ranging in the thousands, it's best to arrive early. So pack a lunch, set up a blanket, and watch the largest range of kites you're likely to see all year. Or bring your own and give it a go.

DATE   First Sunday in March
(check website for rain date)

TIME   10AM – 5PM

LOCATION   Zilker Park, 2100 Barton Springs Rd.

PARKING   Parking can be difficult, so go early or consider taking a shuttle for a minimal fee. Kids and dogs ride free. Note that Barton Springs Rd. is closed during the event.

WEBSITE   www.zilkerkitefestival.com

PHONE   (512) 448-5483

ADMISSION   Free

Additional Resources

Mobile App

The app contains the guide's full entries so you can easily carry the book with you everywhere you go. Special search features make it easy to plan an outing or find destinations nearby, or you can use it as a tool to help you discover new places near your regular haunts. The app makes it simple to look up hours, link to websites, or call the places you're headed. You can find it through the *Exploring Austin with Kids* website.

Book Website: www.ExploringAustinwithKids.com

Austin is a dynamic and rapidly growing city with no shortage of fun to be had. The website will keep you up-to-date with new places to explore, upcoming events, and day trips. You'll also find insider tips, interviews, and relevant ramblings about raising kids in the unique environs of Austin.

Event Calendars

The following websites are a great source of information on current kid events:

Free Fun in Austin lists a number of free activities for every day of the week, along with reviews of many of Austin's best kid-friendly places. *www.freefuninaustin.com/p/event-calendars.html*

Nature Rocks Austin, part of the Children in Nature Collaborative of Texas, posts a monthly calendar of nearby nature-related events. *www.naturerocksaustin.org/calendar*

The Savvy Source lists daily kid events in the Austin area and allows you to search by cost, age, or type of activity. *www.savvysource.com/events/tx/austin*

These print publications pinpoint children's events too and can be picked up at many local grocery stores, or you can find them online:

Austin Chronicle lists weekly kid events in the Community Calendar section. *www.austinchronicle.com/calendar/kids*

Austin Family includes articles on parenting and a monthly calendar of family events and storytimes. *www.austinfamily.com*

Acknowledgments

Thanks

I am indebted to the countless parents, grandparents, and friends who contributed their insights, tips, sharing of secret spots, photographs, and feedback every step of the way. To the friends and family members who went exploring with us, you made our adventures even better! Thank you all for supporting the project so wholeheartedly.

Thanks goes to Jodi Egerton of Write Good Consulting for her editor's eye, and even more so for her South Austin mama insights that added much to the book. And special thanks to Paige Deshong for her support and willingness to help in every aspect of this venture, from its beginning to end.

I could not have found a better partner in designing the book than Monica Thomas. She made collaborating exciting, and I was constantly impressed by her creativity as she would take my rough vision and transform it into a fun, playful reality that fits Austin to a T. Too, I have learned much from Tamara and Tom Dever of TLC Graphics and Narrow Gate Books, whose expertise, professionalism, and enthusiastic support I am so appreciative.

In hindsight, I'd like to thank Stone for his resistance to going to preschool and for wanting to stay at home with Mom. This prompted the search for a guidebook of things we could do together, which led to... well, a bigger project than we anticipated. I am grateful for his agreeing to go "just a few places." Thanks, too, to Emmi for her positive attitude and constant readiness for adventure! I couldn't have done it at all without the constant support—in every way—of Daniel.

Photo Credits

I can't thank Jamie Allen, Jessica Attie, Paige Deshong, and Jen Smith enough for digging through their family photographs to find the best ones for the book. Joy Kling and her sweet daughter kindly allowed me use of family photos taken by Michele Anderson of Pinkle Toes Photography. I appreciate the Blanton Museum of Art's permission to include their photos as well. I am eternally grateful to Deb Lykins of Deborah Lykins Photography and Design for her invaluable artistic expertise and advice. Unless noted, all other photographs were taken by Annette Lucksinger.

Photographs by Jamie Allen:
Austin Independent School District playgrounds, Austin Trail of Lights, Austin Zoo, Barton Creek Greenbelt, City of Austin Splash Pads, Rodeo Austin

Photographs by Jessica Attie:
Barton Springs Pool, Boggy Creek Farm lettuce and sunflowers, BookPeople, Mayfield Park and Preserve

Photographs by Kelly Lynn James, courtesy of the Blanton Museum of Art:
Blanton Museum of Art

Photographs by Paige Deshong:
Día de los Muertos Viva la Vida Fest, Peter Pan Mini-Golf

Photographs by Pinkle Toes Photography:
Big Top Candy Shop, Butler Park

Photographs by Jen Smith:
Pioneer Farms

Index

About the Author

Local author Annette Lucksinger has made her home in Austin, Texas, for the past 15 years. She is a mother of two children, who not only inspired the guidebook but who have proven to be great fellow adventurers. She teaches writing and literature at St. Edward's University.